assert yourself
and change
your life

Suzie Hayman

Copyright © 2011 Suzie Hayman

The moral rights of the author have been asserted.
Database right Hodder Education (makers).

All rights reserved. No part of this publication may be reproduced, stored in
a retrieval system or transmitted in any form or by any means, electronic,
mechanical, photocopying, recording or otherwise, without the prior
permission in writing of Hodder Education, or as expressly permitted by law,
or under terms agreed with the appropriate reprographic rights organization.
Enquiries concerning reproduction outside the scope of the above should be
sent to the Rights Department, Hodder Education, at the address above.

You must not circulate this book in any other binding or cover and you must
impose this same condition on any acquirer.

British Library Cataloguing in Publication Data: a catalogue record for this title
is available from the British Library.

10 9 8 7 6 5 4 3 2 1

The publisher has used its best endeavours to ensure that any website
addresses referred to in this book are correct and active at the time of going
to press. However, the publisher and the author have no responsibility for the
websites and can make no guarantee that a site will remain live or that the
content will remain relevant, decent or appropriate.

The publisher has made every effort to mark as such all words which it
believes to be trademarks. The publisher should also like to make it clear that
the presence of a word in the book, whether marked or unmarked, in no way
affects its legal status as a trademark.

Every reasonable effort has been made by the publisher to trace the copyright
holders of material in this book. Any errors or omissions should be notified in
writing to the publisher, who will endeavour to rectify the situation for any
reprints and future editions.

Hachette UK's policy is to use papers that are natural, renewable and
recyclable products and made from wood grown in sustainable forests.
The logging and manufacturing processes are expected to conform to the
environmental regulations of the country of origin.

www.hoddereducation.co.uk

Typeset by MPS Limited, a Macmillan Company.
Printed in Great Britain by CPI Cox & Wyman, Reading.

Contents

do you want to be assertive?

Most of us would like to be someone who can stand up for ourselves, while not being pushy or unpleasant. Before you can address how you might gain the skills to be assertive in your life, with family and friends, at work and in the world at large, you need to consider what you understand assertiveness to mean. There are upsides to being assertive but there are also disadvantages and these need to be explored for you to be able to take advantage of the tips and strategies we are going to be opening up. Assertiveness is not a natural reaction – our instincts push us towards fight or flight when we are under pressure. Early childhood experiences can push us towards giving in or trying to dominate or manipulate other people instead of being assertive, which is why it can take time and effort, understanding and practice to be able to manage the skills.

If you feel you've suffered years of being overlooked, pushed around, and having your ideas and needs ignored, 'Do you want to be assertive?' may seem like a silly question. Of course you'd like to be able to speak up and speak out! But if you've been finding it hard to make your voice heard, you do need to consider whether one of the reasons is that you have some reservations about being that assertive person. To choose assertiveness, you first have to consider what you feel is meant by being assertive.

Being assertive doesn't mean behaving like some of the people who might have led you to think 'I really need to stand up for myself more!' It does not mean always getting your own way; it does not mean always being in charge. Being assertive isn't when your voice is always loudest or your demands always to the fore. Being assertive is not the same as being dominant, hectoring or bullying. You don't have to be that sort of person to be more in control and more forward than you might be now.

But there are some downsides of being an assertive person. These may be what come to mind when you think of making changes and becoming more forward. And these may be what hold you back. If you are assertive, you:

* must make choices, and acknowledge that not making a choice and doing nothing is a choice in itself
* have to take responsibility for yourself and your choices and stand up and say 'Yes, this is what I think and believe, and do'
* can't make excuses or hide behind other people – you cannot say 'I couldn't help it' or 'They made me do it' or 'Everyone thinks. . .' or 'Of course, it's not what I think. . .'

If you could be a more assertive person, what advantages might you enjoy? You could:

* express your opinions, and feel confident in knowing they are as good as anyone else's
* express your feelings, and know you have as much right to have them as anyone else
* feel in control, and recognize that you have responsibility for your life and your decisions

* make choices, and acknowledge that you can do so
* get some of what you want, knowing that we can't always have everything we desire or need but have a right to ask anyway
* have the right to refuse to do what you don't want.

When you talk about wanting to be more assertive, what you might really mean is:

* How can I get people to listen to and take notice of me?
* How can I stand up to people who push me around?
* How can I have a little more control over my life in general or some situations in particular?

Being assertive is not a natural response, we have evolved to respond to any situation where we feel uncertain or under threat by going into 'fight or flight' mode. If you think you're in danger, a primitive part of your brain tells you to act, at once; step up and attack, or batten down the hatches and get out of there. And to make sure you do so as quickly and efficiently as possible, it floods your body with a cocktail of chemicals that enables you to see clearer, run faster, and fight harder. You may want to wade in there and have it out. Or you may want to freeze and be as invisible as possible, or to run and hide.

Your primitive brain cannot distinguish between little threats and big ones or even real threats and imaginary ones. It's not subtle but it is quick. The effects of the fight or flight impulse can overwhelm you even before you realize you're feeling stressed. You're flooded with the emotions triggered by that primitive and powerful brain. And this emotional flooding often makes rational thought not just hard but impossible. Instead of thinking things through, and acting in control, you find yourself being pushed to be either aggressive – 'fight', or submissive – 'flight'.

Being assertive means learning to overcome this instinctive and often inappropriate reaction. Clearly, when you step in front of a bus or when someone does seek to do violence to you or someone you love, you'll be glad of that rush of strength and speed that allows you to react as is needed. But in most cases freezing or running away or hitting out with words or fists is more likely to get us into a miserable situation than save our lives. Assertive behaviour works so much better, whether at home or at work.

Assertive behaviour helps you and those around you grow and develop. Dominating the people around you tends to be based on short-term rewards and results – the dominant person has their way and feels they have done the right thing because it seems to work.

Being dominant can be beneficial for the person in the lead, but it fails completely to make effective use of the abilities and potential of everyone else. And in fact, it's not much good for the leader either, in the long run. If you only ever get your way because you push, scream and shout, you may never develop real skills – to assess situations and make the best decision, to lead and inspire others to have their say, to change and to adapt. The day someone else stands up and is a bigger bully than you, you're lost. Use this method in families and you may lose out dramatically. Children may vote with their feet, getting as far away from you as they can as soon as they are able. And even if people stay physically close, you may find they absent themselves emotionally, avoiding intimacy with you.

But it's a mistake to think that not standing up for yourself is any better. Being passive is not a good style to live by, either. Again, it has short-term rewards and results – you keep your head down, stay out of the line of fire, have an easy life with little conflict because you always give in. But constantly buckling under isn't good for you or for the people around you. It means never getting your own needs met and that can lead to anger and frustration, meaning neither you nor anyone else you encounter has the chance to learn how to compromise and negotiate – you always step aside for them and let them have what they want.

Using the fight or the flight option is the result of having low self-esteem and low self-confidence. You may not feel you have the right to make your feelings known, you may feel you don't have the skills to stand up for yourself, you may believe that your views and your needs are not as important as anyone else's. But in fact, a similar belief also often fuels those who bully their way through life.

You may think someone behaves like this because they want to and like it. Often, they simply do it because it works and because once they've started to behave this way, everyone around them reinforces the behaviour by letting them get away with it.

Early childhood experiences play an important part in creating this sort of pattern of behaviour. When children find that if they play quietly or ask nicely they are ignored but when they fight and have tantrums and act up they get noticed, then that's the way they will go on behaving. Bullies are victims as well as aggressors so actually deserve sympathy and help to change to more positive ways of interacting. If you are assertive you'll be able to help those people in your life who have self-destructive behaviour patterns to change to more positive ones.

As well as being bossy, you may find yourself being accused of nagging as you work towards becoming assertive. Being assertive is not the same as being a nag. But what is nagging? Sometimes, people accuse us of nagging because they don't want to hear what we're saying – please empty the rubbish, clear the table, do your chores, feed the cat, make that call. . . It's called nagging when really it's 'Yes I know I should be doing that but I don't want to, so I'll try to make *you* feel bad for asking, to stop *me* feeling bad for not doing it!'

Because it is not instinctive behaviour, it takes some work and some effort to pick up and learn to manage the skills of assertive behaviour. Because it is not instinctive behaviour, you don't need to blame yourself or feel bad about not having those skills at present. Because we are thinking and learning beings, the fact that it is not instinctive behaviour does not mean we are stuck forever with being unassertive. Human beings can learn and change – that's what makes us human.

There are two important and, I think, main reasons why choosing to become assertive is the right thing to do. Some people like to make choices for a positive reason – in other words, there's a reason to go forward into making a change. So here's your positive reason: being assertive feels good.

But you may be someone who prefers to make choices on avoidance grounds – you do things to go backwards away from things you don't like. In that case, one very good reason for avoiding *not* being assertive is that being unassertive feels bad!

There are good reasons also for choosing not to be either aggressive or submissive. Being aggressive gets you what you want at other people's expense. They resent you and do not respect you and look for ways of getting away from or getting back at you. It's hard work and you are on your own. Being submissive is also hard work. We let other people do the work but we feel an emotional toll. Never getting what we want is wearing and dispiriting. We resent instead of respecting or loving the people who dominate us, whether family, friends or work colleagues, and never have truly equal or satisfying adult relationships with them. We never bring out the best in them or ourselves.

There is another pattern of behaviour that often comes about when people don't feel they're getting what they want. This is called passive-aggression. Passive-aggression is when we influence and stage-manage people to give us what we want. Classic passive-aggression is the person who says 'Don't mind me – I'll be alright. Yes, you go along and enjoy yourself while I do the clearing up...' It's control by guilt and complaint, and it can work very well. But being passive-aggressive is equally as unsatisfying as being either submissive or aggressive. We may get what we want but it's by underhand means so we can never really admire or like the people we manipulate or ourselves, nor they us. There may be some satisfaction and a sort of empowerment in pulling people's strings but it is unpleasant and we usually don't feel good about ourselves.

Assertiveness will improve your life – it's a far better way of behaving than being either passive or aggressive or passive-aggressive. So how can you begin to become assertive? Here are ten tips we'll be working towards. You need to be able to:

Say it like it is. To make your feelings and wishes known, you're going to learn to be direct and specific. Instead of saying, 'Why do I always have to do everything...', 'You always...', or 'Nobody ever listens to me!', you'll learn to say, 'You left the kitchen in a mess this morning so I'd like you to clear it up now', 'You didn't feed the cat this evening, so I want you to do it now', and 'When

I asked you to finish that report you didn't, so I want you to do it now'. Being direct and specific means the other person knows what you're objecting to, why you're upset and what you want done instead.

Own what you say. When we're being unassertive we often try to palm off our feelings and needs on to someone else. We say 'Everyone is upset with you', or 'We would like...', or 'You don't want to be doing that...'. When you own what you say, you use 'I'. We'll learn how to say 'I'm upset and want to talk about this', 'I would like you to...', and 'I would prefer you to do this...'. Once you own what you say, you get far more of what you need and want.

Walk the talk as well as talk the talk. Your words only convey a fraction of your meaning – your stance says much more. You'll learn to use body language that matches and backs up your words. 'I'm really annoyed with you...' doesn't get the message across if you mumble it with crossed arms while looking down at your feet, or say it with a bright smile.

Give praise. If you want to have influence on other people, for every time you have to pull them up for what they have done wrong, you need to find at least two occasions to thank and praise them. We all want approval and we tend to repeat actions that get us noticed positively. It works far better than trying to get people to do what you want by telling them off when they get it wrong.

Accept compliments. One important aspect of assertiveness is knowing your own worth. And that means when someone gives you a compliment, you say 'Thank you' and accept it, rather than 'Oh, I didn't do anything', or 'What, this old rag! I'm sure my bum looks big in it!' or similar.

Don't make it personal. When dealing assertively with other people, it is behaviour you may object to and wish to change, not the person. Don't say 'You lazy git!' Instead say, 'I'm upset you didn't wash up. I'd like you to do so now.'

Say what you want rather than what you don't want. It works better to tell a child 'We're going shopping. I want you to stay by me in the supermarket and it will really help me if you hold the list and tick off all the things as we find them', than to say 'We're going shopping and I don't want a repeat of last week where you ran up and down the aisles!' People tend to pick up on the words you use, and in that case all the child hears is 'run up and down the aisles'.

Choose the right time. Trying to have a discussion about who takes out the rubbish, or why the kids haven't done the chores, or a workmate's failings in the workplace, is doomed to fail if you pick the moment when everyone is tired or really busy. Say 'We need to talk...' and agree a time to do so.

Choose the right place. Tackling a touchy teen in their own bedroom may make them feel invaded, and thus aggressive. Summoning someone to your room may put them on the defensive. Doing it in front of other people can upset everyone – it's humiliating for the person you're addressing and embarrassing for onlookers. Pick a neutral, quiet spot.

Reward yourself. Give yourself a pat on the back each time you use an assertive response. Do it whether the other person responded well or not.

Nobody changes overnight. You're not going to wake up and be that totally confident assertive person tomorrow. It took time and effort to make you what you are now and it will take time and effort and mindfulness to make yourself what you'd like to be, and what you can happily manage. Don't be anxious that you're somehow going to have to jump, all of a sudden, unprepared and unskilled, into having to manage new habits and new expectations. You'll do it by small and manageable steps, a bit at a time. But one step at a time, you will do it.

Why should you be assertive? Because it's pleasanter than fighting and much nicer than always giving in. Because it's more efficient than either, too. Being aggressive may appear to get you what you want in that instance. What it sets up, however, is an atmosphere in which people do not want to co-operate with you and may work hard at frustrating you. The more aggressive you are, the more aggressive you are driven to be. And the less other people enjoy your company. Being submissive is as bad. The more you let people walk all over you, the more they will take advantage – not just because it's easy to get what they want when you are going to let them, but simply because bowing your head encourages people to kick it.

To be assertive, however, you need to do more than simply learn a set number of tricks and strategies, tips, communication skills and behaviours. You'll find plenty of those in this book and they will prove invaluable to you in becoming a self-assured, confident and charming person to be with. What you also need is a new attitude of mind. To be assertive, you need to accept and recognize and acknowledge that you matter. You have as much right as anyone else to have what you need and want. Not more and certainly not less – but as much.

Assertiveness is, in other words, mainly an attitude of mind with an accompanying set of beliefs about yourself and the world around you. Assertiveness begins by examining the hidden beliefs we have about our worth and the worth of other people. When you have the belief that you are equal to every other person, not better or worse, you can communicate from a position of equality.

2

the tactics we use to get along

Assertiveness may be the most effective strategy when dealing with other people but the reality is, most of us fall into other patterns to get by. We might give in, demand, back off or manipulate to either get our own way, or let other people get theirs. None of these patterns are helpful – they produce stress and tension in you and in those around you. By examining exactly what these tactics are, how they work and what they do to you in the short and long term you can see how you may be choosing or opting to interact at present and how much more effective and pleasant it might be to learn how to be more assertive. Seeing what happens to you when you are submitting, dominating or manipulating other people, and what might happen when you can act assertively, can give you the incentive to learn the skills on offer.

Most people, whether they realize it or not, tend to fall into using one of four main tactics to get by in life. We may:

* give in
* demand
* back off but get your own way by less obvious means
* negotiate.

If you give in you tend towards submissive behaviour. You do not stand up for yourself. You may express your views in a very cautious or mild manner, or you may not express them at all. You probably allow other people to push ahead of you in queues and accept that you always come second or third when sharing. You may go without new clothes or gadgets while other people in your family get what they want. Your birthday or festival present is always the one bought out of the last few pennies – or forgotten or deferred because 'Oh, don't mind me – we can't really afford anything for me!' At work or even in the family, you usually allow others to take credit for work you have done.

You may well resent being used and put upon but you're too biddable to do anything about it. Your general style is to act helpless, be indecisive and look to others to make decisions, to wail, moan and constantly apologize.

What happens when we take the 'easy' route by letting other people set the pace?

You don't get what you want. Submissive people often expect their partner, family or friends to 'just know' what they need and what they want. You expect your boss to realize when you've done all that work and reward you. You expect your partner to know when you're feeling down and could do with some comfort. You expect your family to know when you want them to pull their weight and do their chores. And since they don't – because *no one can read minds* – you live in a constant state of disappointment, and repeatedly have to do all the extra work because everyone else is looking out for themselves, not after you.

You don't avoid confrontation. Confrontation and challenge, arguments and disagreements will still arise. If you are someone who lets other people set the agenda you just run from it when it comes up. It's still going on, but behind your back and out of your sight, whatever is said or resolved does so in ways that are far more of a problem to you, because you're not there to fight your corner.

Rather than avoiding clashes, you may set up situations in which unpleasantness happens more often. Since you don't challenge the difficulty or sort out the reasons behind it, the situation will probably reoccur, and may be far more difficult to sort out because you keep letting it escalate behind your back.

You will lose the ability to manage. The more you avoid difficult situations or people, the more you convince yourself that you're someone who cannot cope. And you will be right, because you won't learn how to resolve or face up to conflict if you don't practise those skills. Your ability to cope will decrease and your self-esteem and self-respect will get lower and lower. Your relationships with other people may well become more and more distant and problematical.

You will constantly be disappointed, frustrated and stressed. Instead of avoiding hassle by taking the easy path, in fact you're likely to find your life becoming more difficult. You won't have the skills to cope with any disagreements so they go on around you, continuously putting you under pressure.

Your relationships with colleagues, friends and family may also deteriorate. You may feel always letting them have their way will endear you to them and gain their approval. In fact, most people find nothing quite as frustrating as having a colleague, friend or family member who always says 'Oh, I don't know – you choose. Don't mind me – you go ahead and make the decision.' You not only make them do all the work, which is tiring and stressful, but you push them into being selfish and even into being bullies.

What's the pay-off of being submissive?

In the short term you:

Avoid conflict. A pay-off for letting other people have their way and sidelining our own is that we avoid arguments. Being passive and submissive can feel like a very simple and effortless route. You can honestly boast that you and your family, your friends, your colleagues, never have a cross word or a disagreement, and that can seem encouraging. Another pay-off of staying quiet about your needs or wishes may also be that you can feel downtrodden and abused. Many people would see that as undesirable. In fact, you can find a certain satisfaction in it – at least it's a predictable outcome. If you look for and work towards the positive result of being heard, you might feel that for all that hard work you only get a percentage of times that your effort is rewarded. If you never try, one advantage is that you get exactly what you expect – 100 per cent hit rate on being right and getting nothing. It can seem easier to play the martyr than to take steps to be heard.

Avoid taking responsibility. By avoiding taking responsibility, you can rest comfortably in the knowledge that you'll never be called to account, never be blamed, never have to explain yourself because it's never your fault. Taking the back position can seem a very safe place to be.

The long term pay-offs of being passive and submissive can be less acceptable. While the immediate pay-offs can seem comfortable, protecting you from conflict and accountability, in the long run it can become distressing.

In the long term you:

Lose even more self-esteem, confidence and worth. The more you avoid conflict, the scarier raised voices, disagreements and anger become. Your tolerance for conflict may go down so even the slightest difference can make you panic. The more you avoid it, the less able you feel you are in managing or resolving any such clash – your self-esteem, your confidence and your feelings of self-worth may consequently reduce. And it's not just in dealing with rows you may lose self-confidence – you may come to see yourself as someone who simply 'can't manage' in many areas.

Build resentment. You may find yourself becoming more resentful of the people you lean on. Since their choices may not be to your advantage, or taste, you may increasingly lose patience with their always taking charge. And they may resent you. Even in a partnership or a family, you might be seen as a freeloader or a drag – someone who gains from the hard work they do without doing your bit. You may not realize or notice all the efforts other people have to make to cover for you.

Suffer stress-related medical problems. People who constantly put themselves at the back of the queue may also find that always giving way, even if you're scared or unused to doing anything else, can become wearing. You may find panic attacks and other stress-related difficulties can develop and increase the more you duck your head and hide behind others.

Aggressive behaviour

If you demand, you lean towards aggressive behaviour. Aggressive behaviour tends to show little or no concern for other people's ideas, feelings and needs. If you are being aggressive your actions may be bossy and arrogant, and help you get your way by bulldozing others. Aggression goes with being intolerant, opinionated and overbearing. An aggressive person gets along by insisting on their rights using anger, threats and sometimes even open violence to be on top. If you tend towards being aggressive you may feel strong and in control, and nod towards the fact that you make the choices and call the shots to justify your behaviour. Your general style is to be in control, decisive, and to raise your voice so everyone hears what you want, what you think and what you expect.

What happens when we take the route of always setting ourselves above and in front of other people?

You get what you insist on. However, it may not always be what you need or even want. By setting the pace you deny those around you the chance to think for themselves and to co-operate with you and between themselves. Aggression stifles innovation – everyone is too busy trying to follow instructions and please the aggressor to have time to think around the issues and come up with their own ideas.

You live in a state of frequent confrontation. Telling people what to do, refusing to listen to their points of view, means you constantly have to assert yourself and your position, and take steps to make sure other people do not win over you. Aggression tends to be met with aggression, so you spend much of your time going up against other people and beating them down. One fight tends to lead to another since aggression does not solve problems, it simply steamrollers over opponents on each occasion, leaving new problems to arise, or the same problem to come up when the other person feels able to try again.

You limit your ability to learn and to develop. Since aggression appears to work, people who use it tend not to learn other strategies – negotiation, compromise, discussion and consensus. This prevents both the aggressor and those around them learning and developing those skills and any other new approaches. Sooner or later they may run out of steam or meet a bigger and more aggressive opponent, and then find they are stuck.

You put yourself under enormous stress. Constantly having the 'fight' button on is exhausting and no matter how much adrenaline and arrogance pushes you forward, the effort needed to maintain this behaviour can have damaging effects on emotional and physical health.

Your relationships with colleagues, friends and family may be unsympathetic. However much such behaviour is apparently admired in business circles as being 'can-do' and effective, in fact it has severe limitations. With family and friends it is not only ineffective but harmful. People may tolerate you but not love you, live with you but not accept you, respect you but not like you. And in fact, in society at large the 'respect for a strong personality' is beginning to give way to dislike of a bully.

The pay-offs for being aggressive seem pretty obvious. In the short term you:

Have a sense of power. By being aggressive, you are the top of the tree and are in control. Nobody pushes you around, nobody makes you do anything you don't want to do and everybody does what you choose. You might feel that any dissent and disagreement in your family and at work are minimized because you know best and lay down the rules. In fact, you may feel justified in thinking that by putting down your foot, arguments seem to be held at bay, since if you're aggressive enough, nobody answers back and all seems peaceful.

Get what you want. People who use aggression are confident that they have their needs fulfilled, and that they can also help other people to avoid wasting time and effort in dithering and time-consuming discussion by getting straight to the point and doing what they have decided.

Take the lead and get the credit. Using aggression usually means that when things work out you can claim the glory. Of course, being on top also means if things go wrong you can point the finger at someone else and make it their fault, not yours.

The long-term pay-offs of being aggressive can be less acceptable. While the immediate pay-offs can seem comfortable, putting you in control, in the long run it can become distressing. In the long term you:

Need to maintain a constant level of stress and pressure. Living with daily conflict can give you a tolerance for it, so that anger and fighting seem normal. You and all around you may assume that a raised voice is always the way to settle any disagreement. You may lose or never develop the skills of discussion, negotiation and compromise, or simply forget to use or apply them.

Increase loneliness. Using aggression usually means you're on your own, making decisions and choices. It's not a co-operative style, which means you may feel resentful at having to be the only one bearing all the responsibility.

Suffer stress-related medical problems. People who constantly put themselves on alert to fight may find it becomes exhausting. Stress-related difficulties can develop and increase the more you push yourself forward and others back.

Rely on being forceful to feel self-esteem, self-confidence and self-worth. When something happens to interrupt the established order, someone who uses aggression may find it hard to maintain their positive feelings about themselves.

Passive-aggressive behaviour

If you back off but get your own way by less obvious means you tend towards passive-aggressive behaviour. Passive-aggressive behaviour tends to be exhibited by those who want their own way but are too low in self-confidence or self-worth to demand it assertively, or aggressively. But that doesn't mean it's any less powerful than out-and-out aggression. Passive-aggressive behaviour may be sarcastic and manipulative and works by making others feel guilty or shamed enough to give the user what they want. Someone may use passive-aggression, not to push their way to the front of the queue, but wander there as if they hadn't noticed there was a queue. Or to sigh and softly complain until you usher them in front of you, or are left feeling ashamed that you were so unreasonable.

People who use passive-aggression may say they would love things to be different – but frustrate any support or suggestions towards change. One reason is that they lack trust in others and have such a negative and passive outlook. The other is that they get what they want far more often than anyone realizes. Their effect on other people, however, is profound. Using complaints and reproaches, sabotage and indirect criticism gets them their own way but at the cost of sowing guilt and discord.

What happens when we use passive-aggression?

Sometimes you do and sometimes you don't get what you want. Using manipulation and behind the scenes moves to try and direct affairs your own way can be surprisingly effective and those using passive-aggression succeed far more often than you might think. However, their behaviour frequently leaves everyone feeling awful.

You avoid outright confrontation. Passive-aggression tends more to niggling arguments in the background about how unfair it is or how nothing goes right but rarely results in obvious quarrels. However, the effect on everyone can be far more distressing and tiring than falling out.

You'll feel negative and defensive. Passive-aggressive behaviour works by the person using it believing they are hard done by, and manoeuvring everyone else to believe so as well.

You'll be trapped in 'learned helplessness'. Passive-aggressive behaviour often results in the user claiming they are ineffectual and incompetent. And the more you tell other people, and yourself, you can't do it, the more that becomes a self-fulfilling prophecy.

You will be stuck. By never communicating your needs or asking for other people's you may miss the fact that you could get a lot of what you want in far less destructive ways. Passive-aggressive behaviour is inefficient and delays any resolution of a problem.

People using passive-aggressive behaviour tend to come across as stubborn and sullen, and colleagues, friends and family may find it hard to sympathize or co-operate with someone using it. Being manipulated is unpleasant and frustrating.

What are the pay-offs of being passive-aggressive?

In the short term you:

Feel safe. People who use passive-aggression usually come from families in which honest expression of feelings was forbidden. This tends to teach children to repress and deny their feelings and to use other means to express their frustration or anger and get their needs met. Manipulating those around them and denying their own feelings and needs makes them feel in control and protected.

Get what you want. You won't ask for what you want or express your real feelings to get what you need, but somehow you end up avoiding doing stuff you don't want to do and having people fall in with your schemes, in spite of themselves.

Keep out of the line of fire. By often neglecting your responsibilities you may get criticized for not doing as much as you should, but you also avoid being held to task. And by leading from behind, by getting people to do what you want by manipulation and suggestion, you can always blame the people who appeared to be in the lead if it goes wrong.

Play the victim. You can gather great sympathy and support from people who don't know you very well by always framing events in your favour.

The long-term pay-offs of being passive-aggressive can be less acceptable. In the long term you:

Are always on the edge. Using passive-aggression takes a lot of energy and work, all aimed at blaming others for shortcomings and ducking out of responsibilities. You may spend a lot of time feeling victimized, being unable to trust others, feeling sulky and resentful.

Build your self-esteem, self-worth and self-confidence on shaky foundations. If you convince yourself that it's never your fault but always other people's, that you are hard done by and it's only bad luck that holds you back, you risk one day discovering that it's actually down to you. You may need to work hard to continue to convince yourself it's everyone else's fault. And, of course, you never have the chance to be in control of your own self-esteem.

Are alone. Passive-aggressive behaviour tends to go hand in hand with a distrust of authority and a fear of being close to people – either of having to step up and be compared, or of relying on them.

Can be stuck and at a loss. Passive-aggression is about steering clear of anger – about having been taught, as a child, that anger is unacceptable. But we all feel anger – it's how we deal with it that matters. Most children learn to cope with negative feelings – to accept them, work with them and manage them. If what you have learned is to bury anger and hostility you never grow beyond it – anger is constantly under the surface and you can't gain the skills to deal with it. What people with passive-aggressive behaviour are doing is dealing with feelings like a toddler and either being overwhelmed by them or hiding from them. This might be acceptable and understandable behaviour in a young child, but highly dysfunctional in an adult.

Suffer stress-related medical problems. Constantly suppressing anger is not good for your health. It tends to come out in health issues for the person suppressing it, and in less obvious ways for everyone around them. People suppressing anger tend to let it leak out in less open but even more destructive behaviour – sarcasm, criticism, sullenness, complaints.

If you negotiate, you tend towards assertive behaviour. If your behaviour is assertive you stand up for yourself and your rights, but you do not do so at the expense of others. You express your ideas, feelings and needs, while at the same time recognizing that other people also have the right to express and pursue their own. You may allow other people in front of you in the queue, when you're not in a hurry and someone else is. When it matters, you will firmly but quietly take a stand. Assertive people are direct and honest. They accept other people for what they are, take responsibility for their own actions but not for other people's, and are flexible and spontaneous.

Being assertive means being able to put your foot down firmly while not trampling on other people's rights. Assertive behaviour negotiates and reaches workable compromises. Assertive people have confidence in themselves and are positive, while at the same time understanding other people's points of view.

What happens when you are assertive?

You don't always get what you want. Assertive people are clear about what they want and need, think and feel. They don't expect anyone – partner or family, friends or colleagues – to be able to read their minds so they say what they mean and mean what they say. At work, they will take responsibility and own up to mistakes but equally will claim credit for what they have done. Since they will also listen to other people and their needs and wants, this doesn't always mean getting what they want completely and every time – sometimes a compromise is necessary. It means, however, that they will always feel they have heard and been heard and so feel satisfied and fulfilled, knowing their needs are being mostly met.

You avoid confrontation. That does not mean you avoid challenge. Assertive people will discuss and face up to contrary views but they will do it in the spirit of co-operation, with negotiation and compromise. This means it is not an argument but an arbitration, where all views are given weight and respected. An assertive person may still say 'I'm the boss/I'm the parent and the buck stops with me', but they will do it having taken other ideas on board. By helping other people to feel respected and listened to, assertive behaviour counteracts the need for confrontation.

You feel skilled. Assertive behaviour takes some practice and takes some effort to apply but it leaves you and all around you feeling satisfied and in control.

It works! Using assertive behaviour is slower than using aggression, where you get what you want at once without debate, or submission, where you give in. It saves time in the long run, however, since assertive behaviour leaves everyone feeling OK about the situation and so more co-operative, and that tends to be far more effective.

Your relationships with family, friends and colleagues benefit. Using assertive behaviour results in everyone having their say and being heard. It may not mean you always get what you want, nor give all those around you exactly what they want every time. What it does mean is that all of you get much of what you need most of the time, and that leads to everyone feeling content.

In the short term you:

Build self-confidence, self-worth and self-esteem. Being assertive 'adds value'; it makes you feel good about the way you are treating other people, and does the same for them.

Move from win/lose to win/win. When you are assertive you don't always get exactly what you want when you want it, so you don't always win outright. However, your behaviour doesn't force other people into being either winners or losers either. Assertive behaviour leads to everyone sharing and compromising so that you all get some of what you want at some point, thus making you all winners in the end.

Take responsibility and feel good about it. Taking responsibility means sometimes having to shoulder the blame when things go wrong. But it also means being in the forefront with achievements.

Avoid conflict. Being assertive often means having to face up to disagreements and differences. But by dealing with them with confidence and skill, they become discussions rather than descending into quarrels.

In the long term you:

Hone more skills. Being assertive means using all sorts of skills to make your point and listen to those of others. The more you use such skills, the more of them you learn and perfect. Assertiveness skills are also 'transferable' – you can use them with family, friends, colleagues and in the world at large.

Become more effective in relationships, family and work. Being assertive fosters strong and mutually respectful relationships with those around you. Assertive behaviour allows all of you to make feelings known, feel heard by and listen to other people, have your needs met and help meet the needs of the people with whom you interact.

3

knowing your rights

Having an appreciation of your rights or what is due to you is key to becoming more assertive. Being either submissive or dominating often comes from not appreciating what you can and should, and what you can't and shouldn't, claim. Assertiveness rests on knowing that you are as good as but not better or worse than anyone else, and that you have every right to express opinions and be listened to. Being assertive is recognizing you can make mistakes or say no to requests and knowing how to assess when something is, or is not, your responsibility and acting accordingly. It also rests on steering the course between putting yourself forward or first and having a care of other people's needs and wishes. Once you can understand your rights you can prioritize, putting your foot down about issues that you judge to be important or letting some things go.

'I know my rights!' is most likely to be the cry of someone using aggression rather than assertion. But knowing or, more accurately, understanding and acknowledging your rights is actually an important part of being assertive. Whether you realize it or not, at the root of much non-assertive behaviour is a range of beliefs about your lack of rights. Before you can start gaining assertiveness skills and putting them into action you first need to consider what you should expect of yourself, and what others can expect of you.

What do you feel you're entitled to? Whether it's in our intimate relationships or with our family, with friends, with colleagues or in the world at large we all proceed with some assumptions about what we think is due to us. These assumptions set the way we relate with others, and feel about ourselves. Do any of these sound familiar? Are they things you might say?

* 'If someone asks me to do something I must have a good excuse before I can say no.'
* 'I must do things well or not do them at all.'
* 'My family should come before me.'
* 'I feel so stupid when I don't know something.'
* 'I don't like giving my opinions – what I say isn't important.'
* 'Oh no, I wouldn't try that – something may go wrong!'
* 'What other people think about me is really important to me.'
* 'When family members or friends or colleagues make a request, I ought to do as they ask.'
* 'People would think I'm rude or bossy if I stand up for my rights.'
* 'If people I know have problems I feel it's up to me to do something about them.'
* 'I'd rather give in than have a fight.'

If you answered yes to just one of those, this chapter is for you. Two or more and you really need to read on!

You, just as much as any other person, have certain rights. This doesn't mean you should be in a dominant position over others, or that you should be able to make other people do what you want. What it does mean, however, is that you need to recognize that you have just as much claim as anyone else to what is due to you. You deserve just, morally good, legal, proper and fitting treatment, as does everyone around you. To become assertive you should first recognize that.

What rights does an assertive person lay claim to?

The right to say no. This is perhaps the most fundamental of all. We are, every day, surrounded by responsibilities, expectations and demands. You may agree that some of these are down to you, some will be none of your business. But do you have the ability, do you feel you have the right, to say 'no' to any of them? Being assertive means knowing when you can, and that you should, say 'No, I'm not doing that.' The skill, of course, is in being able to do so while keeping yourself and, where possible, other people, from feeling bad about it.

The right not to have to give excuses for our behaviour. Along with the right to say no, is the understanding that we don't have to explain ourselves when we do say it. If you go into a long and involved excuse, what you are actually saying is 'You have a right to know why I'm saying no.' Handing over that right to know then implies 'You have a right to my time and attention' and following on from that 'Which means you have the right to come back and knock down my excuses and get what you want!' Which is what usually happens when we give excuses – the other person immediately tries to work around them. When you say no, you have your reasons; you don't have to explain them. Not doing so sends the powerful message 'I have assessed the situation and made my decision as is my right to do.'

The right to be listened to. We should expect other people to hear what we are saying. That's not the same as their having to fall in line with us or be swayed by us – that's their responsibility to decide. But everyone should have the right to expect other people to listen to what they say, to take it on board and value what is said as being an expression of their feelings and opinions.

The right to express personal opinions. You don't know everything – you may not know much – but everyone has a right to say what they think and feel. Your opinions are your own and you have just as much right to own them, and to claim space to voice them, as anyone. Other people have the right to question your facts and debate the basis of your opinions and beliefs; what no one has the right to do is to stop you thinking or saying them or to deny that your opinions are yours, and have value for that reason.

The right to say 'I don't know'. We don't always have an answer or an opinion. Being assertive is knowing when to declare lack of knowledge and to know there's nothing wrong in doing so. It doesn't diminish you in any way to have areas where you lack knowledge or certainty, nor to say so.

The right to give and receive feedback. Feedback is when we respond to what someone has said or asked or done, or listen to what other people have to say about us and our behaviour. Giving and receiving feedback is an important part of communicating, negotiating and compromising, all vital skills in assertive behaviour. You need to feel free to offer feedback, and to ask for it, to be able to be assertive.

The right to make mistakes. Assertive behaviour understands that we all make mistakes – it's normal and that's how we learn. Making mistakes is not a sign of moral weakness or stupidity – it's simply because we can't know everything and have to learn and practise skills. So one important aspect of assertiveness is knowing that mistakes are OK and not to be avoided, glossed over or excused. You make a mistake, take the lesson and move on.

The right to change my mind. Politicians are particularly fond of refusing to back down, or denying it when they do make a U-turn as if a change of mind shows weakness or foolishness. In fact, changing your mind means you have weighed up new evidence and decided it should affect your position. It does not show an inability to know your own mind – on the contrary, it shows an ability to assess, consider and evaluate and it is an important right to claim.

The right to say 'that's not my responsibility'. We all have responsibilities – things that are ours to do and to be accountable for. But it's very easy to find yourself taking over other people's jobs – maybe because we feel to get them done well and on time it has to be down to us. It's equally easy to respond to other people's demands or requests to do things for them and take the burden off their shoulders. We often feel bad or selfish if we don't accept other people's responsibilities as our own. Being assertive is knowing when and how to say 'No – that's yours, not mine. If you don't do it, it doesn't get done. That's not my business.'

The right to do things in my own way. Sometimes, what we do and how we do it can be done differently and maybe more efficiently. It's important to be able to say 'No, this is how I want to do this' and to be heard and left alone. You may, after reflection, change your mind – that's up to you. But what is essential is to be able to make that choice.

The right to be given respect. Whether other people agree with you or violently disagree, we should all respect each other's opinions and right to make our own decisions. Part of being assertive is to know that you have the right to be respected and accorded value.

The right to expect certain standards from other people. You cannot insist that other people do what you say or act as you want them to, just as you have the right to ask them not to expect you to fall in with their demands. But you do have the right to expect them to be respectful, responsible and honest, as you would like to be to them.

The right to be consulted when decisions might have an impact on me. Whether at home, with friends or at work, we should expect other people to take us and our wishes and needs into account when they make plans that affect us too.

The right to take appropriate risks. Sometimes we opt for the tried and tested, safe and easy route. But sometimes it's vital to step outside our comfort zone, take some risks and try something different, whether in our private or work lives. Just because you are a parent, a partner, somebody's child or somebody's employee or employer, doesn't mean you should always do what is expected and safe. We need to know we can take some risks sometimes, and be able to let other people know it's OK.

How does upholding your own rights work in reality? It's all very well to read about these and think about them in theory, but what do you do when you come up against other people in the big, wide world?

Being assertive is showing appropriate self-interest. You're a member of many communities. You're a member of society, of a family, perhaps of a couple, maybe of a workplace and a friendship group. In all of those groups there are times when it's correct that you think of others and act accordingly. Perhaps you're the one who stands for ages holding open the shop door while people get in out of the rain. Or you drive someone in the family to an event when you'd rather be at home curled up in front of the TV. Or you go to a film you know your partner will love . . . and you won't. Or you give up your day off to help at work when there is a rush on, or meet friends for a drink even though you'll have to catch up the time for something else you had to do. All of those can be a constructive part of your life. But being assertive is knowing when it's time to say 'I have to think of myself here.' Sometimes we need to say no or ask for a different arrangement to suit our needs too.

One of the key points in asserting yourself and claiming your rights is to consider your priorities. You undermine yourself and don't send clear messages about where you wish to stand and how others should respond to you if you have these confused. You need to think about what you feel is non-negotiable, what you might compromise and what is actually unimportant. You stand a much better chance of getting what you need and want if your requests are appropriate. Using all your weight on a matter that is actually unimportant means when it comes to what should be a non-negotiable issue you can't make the distinction.

Most of the problems we fall into come about because we try so hard to please other people – our family, our friends, our employers. It dates back to wanting to please and be appreciated by our parents. One good tip for passing on assertiveness to your children is to help them cultivate the habit of looking to themselves for approval before they look elsewhere. If you only think well of yourself when your worth is reflected through other people's eyes, you are forever at the mercy of their interests. Of course, some of the people you encounter will want the best for you and be sympathetic, kind and enabling. But some will give you approval only as it suits them – when what you are doing pleases them rather than benefits you. Think of the parents who only say their child is being good and acceptable when that child is doing what they want, rather than what might be right for the child. Think of the partners who only say they love you if you're doing what they say. Or the friends who only applaud you if you're falling in with their plans. What we need is children who can answer the question 'Are you pleased with what you have done? Are you satisfied and full of self-worth?' with a YES! And you need to be able to do that for yourself, too. If you didn't have the good fortune to be helped to be proud of yourself when young you can do it now.

responsibilities

Having looked at rights, we need to consider and recognize the responsibilities that go with them. Assertive behaviour goes hand in hand with accepting change, and with taking on duties, and it is fear of these that can hold us back. Change is always hard and difficult, even when it is change that we know will be beneficial. Living in a risk-averse culture we are often tempted to leave well alone and stay as we are rather than gambling with something different. 'What is the worst that could happen – the change or stay as you are?' will be the question to consider. As well as these issues, we explore who stops you making changes in your life – not the people you might think are oppressing you but yourself, since the truth is that nobody can do anything to you or make you do anything you don't want to do, without your consent.

We've looked at the rights you can lay claim to, and considered the importance of recognizing you have them. On the surface, anyone might think that's enough to make becoming assertive very appealing. After all, who can resist being given such advantages, and who can believe **not** having or exercising your rights is an attractive proposition?

But there are some downsides to standing up for yourself. We need to explore them because it's the recognition or realization that there are other sides to this that hold you back, even if you haven't realized that is what is happening.

With rights go responsibilities – and it's these that can make taking action and becoming assertive difficult. If you become assertive and claim your rights, you can no longer hide behind excuses. 'I was late because I couldn't get away' is not something an assertive person says. Nor can you blame other people – 'It's all your fault' can no longer be in your vocabulary. Becoming assertive might make you feel uncomfortable because you have to stick your head above the parapet – you have to take decisions and stand by them. There are pay-offs to taking on responsibilities and making changes. Pay-offs, however, can be felt to be both negative and positive. We'll need to confront our own fears and anxieties about becoming assertive before we can go any further.

We live in a society that is changing at a rate probably never seen before. When I was growing up parents and children were forever at loggerheads because we'd get home from school and then hog the family phone talking to our friends. Now, it's mobile phones and the internet, and a type and expectation of almost full-time connectivity that our grandparents would have believed was the stuff of science fiction. I could name some social networking sites that most of us over 25 never even dreamed of when we were kids – but by the time you read this they may well have been superseded by the next new thing!

What initiatives such as these have meant is that most of us have had to get used to things rapidly evolving and becoming different. Change has always been something we struggle with, whether a change for the better or the worse. The stress around making adjustments to our lives seems more acute now since it is so common. But it's how we view change and either embrace it, try to avoid it or become downright terrified of it, that can affect how you manage. We have to make more and more effort to keep up, yet we are constantly bombarded with messages that tell us the new and the desirable is labour-saving, easy and simple. It's a contradiction that can make people stressed. Far from being exciting and helpful, we can find making any alteration in our lives and our behaviour is difficult and stressful.

We are a 'risk-averse' culture. Most of us feel meddling may make things more, not less, difficult, so it's far better to stay with a known quantity and keep things as they are. We don't like taking risks, in case it is for the worse, and this often works against us seeking change. We may hold back from acting and becoming more assertive because:

* I could make a fool of myself, trying to assert myself and failing.
* I could upset other people by trying to get above myself.
* If I tried to change and didn't manage it, I might make my life more difficult than it already is.
* You shouldn't meddle, because you'll make it worse.
* If it ain't broke don't fix it.

The problem is that if you're reading this, it is broke and it does need fixing! Take the risk – what is the worst that can happen? You might fear you'd fail and feel awful or that people would laugh at you or take even more advantage of you because you tried and were unsuccessful. In fact, the worst that can happen is that you're just the same as you were. So why not try, because if it can't get worse, it may get a whole lot better?

What we imagine is going to happen if we make changes is far worse than the reality. How many times have you geared yourself up to doing something, avoiding it or dreading it, and then afterwards say 'Oh, that wasn't so bad after all!' Our fears are frequently out of proportion to the actual situation, and we simply don't factor in the benefits that will come from going ahead. The worst case scenario of trying is often this:

* You tried and didn't manage it. . . this time. It takes time and effort to change yourself, your beliefs and your behaviour. You can always try again, a bit at a time, slowly over a period. One setback is only that – a setback, not a failure.
* You tried and didn't manage it. . . but learned something. Each time you make an attempt you gain valuable hints as to what went wrong and what you could do next time to make it work.
* You tried and didn't manage it. . . but gave everyone else something to think about. When you step outside the box you alert those around you to the fact that you aren't prepared to go on as you have done up to then. They may not take you so much for granted any more, especially when you try again.

That's the worst case scenario. The actual reality is likely to be this:

* You tried and were pleasantly surprised at how much easier it was than you thought.
* You tried and realized a few small changes could add up to big differences.
* You tried and found those around you were encouraging.
* You tried and found although it took effort, the results were worth it.

Being scared of change and of taking on responsibility for yourself is a natural anxiety. One way of dealing with it is to recognize that being scared isn't that awful an emotion to experience. Indeed, sometimes we deliberately court it and enjoy it – what are horror films and roller-coasters about other than being ways of making us frightened for fun? We seek out frights sometimes because the reaction we have to fear – an adrenaline rush, pounding heart, sweaty palms – is exhilarating. Overcoming fear and working with it and through it is an essential part of personal development. If you avoid something that frightens you, the fear does not go away – in fact, it can grow. If you face it, you can begin to confront it and conquer it. By facing a fear, you can remove its power to intimidate you and so build up your self-confidence and self-esteem.

This is the big secret of being assertive:

Nobody can do to you what you refuse to have done.

Another person cannot make you do anything, unless you agree to do it. Another person cannot take away your power, unless you give it to them.

When you are late for a meeting because someone else makes you stay, or babysit for a friend when you have other things you want to do, or go out when you'd rather stay in that night, unless you've been kidnapped, tied up, had your car keys confiscated or the door locked on you, the other person is not making you do anything: you are.

But of course, in the back of your mind, you may already know this. And that's one of the first and vital choices about becoming assertive. Because being a victim, being someone whom other people push around and tell what to do, can actually be quite a comfortable, safe position. By handing over responsibility for yourself you may feel secure and blame-free — someone else has to shoulder the work and the culpability. There are upsides to being looked after. In considering becoming more assertive you need to recognize, acknowledge and accept why you may have chosen to be non-assertive, and what you will need to both lose and gain in making new choices.

5

beliefs and values

Your beliefs about yourself and those around you can hold you back from being assertive. We'll look at ways of challenging the limiting beliefs so many of us hold about ourselves so you can decide which beliefs you may want to keep and which to discard. If you feel you're incompetent, incapable and that everyone else has more rights than you it can be hard to feel you have a right to stand up for yourself. Negative beliefs can lock you into unhelpful patterns and these can be difficult to escape. We'll explore practising affirmative thoughts to raise self-esteem and confidence and break those patterns. We'll also look at changing the language we use from the negatives of can't, don't, mustn't to the positive of can, do and should – altering language can be surprisingly powerful and effective in effecting a change in behaviour.

In the journey to becoming assertive you may well find your beliefs about yourself can hold you back. One of the important steps to being able to stand up for yourself is to examine what beliefs and values you hold, how they may be affecting you and what you can do to change them.

What sort of beliefs hamper and hinder you? Look at the following and see if any of them sound familiar:

* I'm no good at anything.
* Everyone else always seems to know what they're doing.
* I don't deserve it.
* People don't change.
* My needs aren't as important as other people's.
* My partner and kids should always come first.

Negative beliefs such as these undermine us. Before you can even begin to practise assertive behaviour you need to change the voice you hear telling you what you are, and are not, capable of to a positive one. If you don't value yourself, it's hard for other people to value you.

It becomes far easier to act assertively once we have a sense of our own self-worth. Self-esteem and self-confidence are tightly bound up with an ability to know what we should expect to be due to us. You can act assertively if what you believe about yourself is that:

* I have many skills and abilities.
* I am deserving.
* I can change my behaviour and so can you.
* My needs are as important as, but not more or less than, other people's.

In contrast, acting unassertively proceeds from a low sense of self-worth and from low self-esteem and confidence. But there is one important thing to remember when you are feeling put upon and hard done by. Eleanor Roosevelt once said 'No one can make you feel inferior without your consent.' And she was right.

There is no doubt that the beliefs that other people instil in you are powerful and important. If you've been brought up being told, at worst, you're useless or, at best, 'Don't worry, dear, you can't expect to go far. . .' it can be difficult to fight against those beliefs. Other people's lack of faith in you rapidly translates to an absence of conviction in yourself. You may not even remember it started with other people; by now, it's ingrained and part of you. Every time you try and fail you confirm in yourself your lack of ability. What you miss is that your failures may occur because you don't have any confidence, or that they aren't actually failures at all but you only seeing the negative. What you miss, most of all, is that you give away your strength.

You need to learn to talk to yourself in the way you would like someone else who wants to be supportive and effective to talk to you – a good friend, a professional counsellor, a loving and caring parent. What you need is for that voice to aid you in banishing obstructive thoughts and replacing them with helpful ones: to be affirming, encouraging, challenging and supportive.

Each day, when you are getting ready in the bathroom take a few minutes to look at yourself and tell yourself a few new home truths. Go through the following, and choose what best fits your needs, depending on what the nasty voice is telling you at present:

I'm no good at anything. Oh yes you are! Everyone has at least one thing they do really well. And most of us have a whole range of things, if we only recognized it or were prepared to brush aside the nay-saying and get on with it. Go on – ask yourself what do you do well, and see what pops into your mind. It can be something silly and apparently trivial or something really important. Once you begin to look, you'll find there is a range of things you do that you can be justifiably proud of. What should you be telling yourself? *I am good at many things – I should be proud of my skills, and on the look out for more to add to the list*.

Everyone else always seems to know what they're doing. They may seem to but that doesn't mean they do. We all bluff and cover up and when you're convinced you're all at sea and everyone else has it sussed, the likelihood is that everyone else is just as uncertain about themselves, and just as convinced you know what you're doing. What should you be telling yourself?

I'm the same as everyone else – sometimes we know what we're doing and sometimes we don't. So what?

I don't deserve it. When you want something, or when good things happen, this unkind voice may tell you that you haven't earned it or aren't worthy of it. But you have and you are – trust me! You work hard, you look after other people and you make sure they get what they merit. It's time to extend that generosity to yourself. What should you be telling yourself? *I deserve good things – I've earned them!*

People don't change. It's easy to feel you're stuck as who you are, and that other people will always be the way they are. None of that is true. You can't change other people but you can certainly choose to act differently, feel differently and be a different person – and so can others. What should you be telling yourself? *I'm not stuck – I can change if I want to.*

My needs aren't as important as other people's. So what makes them so special and you so ordinary? Someone may have said so sometime in your life and others may have never contradicted this so you've accepted it. But it simply isn't true. Your needs have equal weight with everyone else's and you have just as much right to be considered – and that's a fact. What should you be telling yourself? *My needs are as important as anyone else's.*

My partner and kids should always come first. Often we have to put children first – they're dependent on us, we chose to have them and we're the grown-ups so we have the capability to put our own needs on hold until theirs are satisfied. And there are times when we may choose to care for our partner and cater for them before ourselves. But sometimes we should be first in the queue. Children need to learn how to wait their turn and that parents have needs too – that's an important and healthy lesson for them to learn. And putting a partner first should be a reciprocal or give-and-take exchange – they care for you as often as you care for them. If you don't look after yourself you may not have the energy to look after them when they need you, so if for no other reason, sometimes you need to put yourself first. What should you be telling yourself? *Sometimes, I should come first.*

Your aim will be to change unhelpful thoughts – 'I can't do this', 'I'm bad at that' – into helpful ones – 'I have a talent for this', 'I excel at that'. Looking at the power of the language you often use can be instructive.

When we're not feeling positive about ourselves, the language we use reflects this. What we say, particularly to describe ourselves and our abilities, is overwhelmingly negative. How often do you find yourself saying 'can't', 'don't', 'won't', 'mustn't', 'oughtn't'?

Or even using lukewarm statements when people ask you if you'd like to do something or to describe your abilities, such as 'okay', 'all right', 'go on then', 'I suppose so'.

And even when you do say 'Yes' or 'I'll do that' or 'I can...', find yourself qualifying it with 'but...', 'however', 'except...'. 'I'll help you make tea but I'm awful at making scones', 'I can write that report for you however I won't be able to manage the maths', 'I'll arrange the meeting except I can't speak myself'. If you need some help or have something extra to say, a better word to use, which is positive, is 'and': '....and I'll need some support at making the scones/doing the maths/making the speech'. Use 'and', and all of a sudden, you can do it. You're not promising anything you can't handle, you are asking for a supportive hand, but most important of all, you're telling them and yourself you can do it.

Purposefully changing your language may seem artificial, ineffective or trivializing the situation, but it can have powerful effects. When some companies brought over the American habit of saying 'Have a nice day' to everyone it may have seem forced and unnatural but most people now recognize it does work. Having it said may be a matter of company policy, but it does alter the atmosphere for the better.

Statements such as 'I can't', 'I ought', 'I never', 'I don't deserve', 'No one likes me' limit your belief in yourself and your ability to change and develop. As we've already discussed, that can seem like an advantage – it means you can avoid taking on responsibility. But the risks are what make you unhappy and uncomfortable because negative language can result in your getting stuck in unhelpful patterns.

How do you know that? When you say 'can't,' what evidence do you have? If you've not been able to do something in the past, that's no reason to conclude you'll never be able to manage it. A bit of confidence, a bit of practice or a bit of support would all have you learning a skill or displaying a talent that you might not have realized or recognized you had or were perfectly capable of developing. You don't know you *can't* until you've tried without that voice in your head saying 'You're not going to be able to do this.' Replace it with a voice that says 'It may take time and preparation but I can do this' and see what happens.

Can I be specific? We often send out unclear messages when we feel unassertive. We don't just say 'I can't do this' when referring to a particular issue but descend into a general grumble of 'It's all so hard. . .', 'No one ever listens to me. . .', 'What can you do?' When this happens you need to ask yourself 'How?', 'In what way?', 'How do you know?' Requiring yourself to be specific means you often discover the problem is less than you thought, because you can't come up with many – or any – specific examples. You're expecting to be thwarted, and talking yourself into feeling ineffective and incapable.

What stops you? When you say 'don't, won't, mustn't, shouldn't, oughtn't', is it fear that prevents you trying – fear of failure, of humiliation, of being laughed at? Or of having to step up and be judged? Or is it memories, past or present, of someone saying 'You shouldn't do this' or 'We don't do that'? Is it fair? Is it just? Is it someone else's problem you're being landed with here? Maybe someone you know or knew thought these things – why should you? Examine what stops you, carefully and clearly; you may want to push the barrier aside.

What makes you? When you say 'must, ought, should' is it anxiety that pushes you on – are you scared of being scolded or disappointing someone if you don't do this? And, again, is it a realistic, present anxiety or one from your past, still affecting you? There is a difference between things that are truly necessary in our own lives, and those that we continue feeling are our responsibility or have to be done which are hangovers from past guilt or another person's belief. You don't 'have' to do anything – you choose to do them, and sometimes you need to revisit that choice and make new ones.

Who told you that? When you say 'don't deserve, never, always', whose voice do you hear? In most of the negative language or strictures we employ, if we think about it we can hear the voice that originally instilled this belief in us. A family member? A teacher? A colleague, friend, acquaintance? What were their motives in telling us this? It might have been based on care and concern, but is the result protective and helpful, or overprotective and thus unhelpful? Or, once you think it through, might control have been the motive? Or could it be based on something destructive from their own past which they are simply handing on to you, like a toxic parcel? Once you know the voice you can examine the motive behind the advice, but also if it is actually helpful to you. If it isn't, change the voice for your own, telling you something a whole lot more constructive: 'I do deserve; often this is right; mostly it is good. . .'.

Can you think of an example that contradicts? If you're telling yourself you can't, you shouldn't, you never . . . can you think of just one instance when you found your fears were not realized and this was not true? Just one? One is a crack in the dam. If you can come up with a time you managed to be skilful, if you can remember an instance when you achieved, it means the blanket belief that you 'can't' is wrong. And if you did it once you can do it again. And again.

How would it be if you could? Having looked at and examined the negatives holding you back, turn your thoughts forward. Imagine and explore what it might be like if instead of can't, oughtn't, mustn't, your motto was 'I choose to do it, I can do it and I deserve to do it. . .'. Each time a barrier threatens to block your way, visualize what it would feel to you and what the situation could look like if there was no barrier. Think what it would be like if you could. That's the first step towards making it happen.

6

becoming assertive

Becoming assertive is a process which doesn't happen overnight. Assertiveness is a set of skills rather than something we are born knowing, and part of the process may be in unlearning the lessons of being unassertive that we might have picked up in the past. But as we shall explore, not only should you forgive yourself for not knowing those skills now but you can be reassured that they can be learned, little by little. It's worth making the effort because assertiveness is so much more efficient and pleasant than the alternatives. You can learn how to model what you want and reinforce good behaviour in your children instead of putting up with conflict and misunderstanding. Strategies such as using 'I' messages and 'broken record', watching your tone and pitch and your body language, and giving and receiving feedback will all help you hold your own with family and friends and work colleagues.

Becoming assertive is a process that takes time. You weren't born assertive – just needy! Some lucky people learn assertiveness as they learn to walk and talk. They learn as tiny infants that what they need will be given to them. They learn as growing toddlers that sometimes they have to wait their turn and that there are boundaries around their behaviour. Gradually, they learn if they ask firmly but also offer respect and thoughtfulness their needs will be met because they are as important as everyone else – no more, no less. But not all of us are that lucky. Many of us learn not to assert ourselves. Either we learn to fight for everything we feel we need, and become aggressive. Or we learn that it seems easier and more comfortable to knuckle under and be submissive. Or, of course, we learn to get our own way in manipulative, underhand ways.

What you're going to do now is to lose your aggression, submissiveness or passive-aggression and add to the skills of assertiveness you already have. It's taken you many years to reach the place you are now and while it won't take as long to unlearn lessons and take new ones on board, it will take a noticeable period. You may find yourself feeling anxious, in denial, being overwhelmed, depressed, scared, threatened or disillusioned as you make the journey. In time, you'll feel elated, capable and, finally, confident.

Why should you make the time and effort to learn assertiveness?

Being assertive is efficient. It takes so long to beat about the bush or argue. Being assertive involves a straight request or statement of needs – it gets to the point, and with care and respect.

Being assertive gives the other person their space too. They can consider your request – assertive behaviour gives other people time or room to consider, negotiate, reschedule – whatever is needed to align your needs.

Being assertive means no one has to be defensive or apologetic. It's an invitation to deal, not a demand for capitulation.

Being assertive gives everyone else a model to follow.
You're being upfront, stating what you need and making it clear
you would like a reply in kind. Assertive behaviour tends to trigger
assertive behaviour in other people, when they see how it works.
Resentment comes with everything . . . except assertion.

Probably the most important strategy you need to learn to
become assertive is to use 'I'. Sounds odd? Sounds silly? Sounds
easy? It's none of those!

We tend to be brought up to use the impersonal voice. If you
think about it, how many times do you use 'you' or 'we' or 'they'
or 'everyone' instead of I?

We make 'You' statements for several reasons. 'Look what you
made me do' or 'You make me so angry!' blame the other person
for what has happened and let us off the hook. A statement such as
'Everyone thinks you're lazy' avoids taking responsibility for angry
or critical remarks by saying they belong to someone else.

The problem with 'You' statements is that they seldom give
the other person a chance to understand what we're upset about,
how we feel or why, or give them an opportunity to make any
changes. 'You' statements may be a way of not being overwhelmed
by anger or despair. Instead of 'owning' feelings, we hold them at
arm's length: 'One feels like that, doesn't one?', 'That's how you do
it, don't you?'

When being assertive, you need to own what you say. Instead
of these roundabout ways of saying something you make it a direct
statement of your own feelings or thoughts:

> *I felt too embarrassed to say anything.*
> *Sorry, I can't come.*
> *I'm really unhappy with you.*
> *I think you're wrong.*

Owning what you say is a big step since it can go against
years of teaching. We're often taught as children that saying 'I'
is arrogant or selfish or demanding. You might have been told
'I want doesn't get' or 'It's not all about you, you know!' The habit
you might have got used to is distancing yourself from requests or

comments. You don't make direct requests – I want/need/would like this – because you're afraid of showing vulnerability or of being turned down. And you don't make honest statements of how you feel – I don't like that/I don't agree with that – in case it attracts scorn or criticism, or upsets people. It can take some time to get into the habit of using 'I' statements, which isn't surprising. Most of us have had a lifetime of being told it's selfish or big-headed to say 'I'. But the more you use them, the more you'll find they work and help you and the other person feel good about the exchange.

Being assertive is standing up for and by what you feel, think and mean. When you use an 'I' statement, you:

* are aware of your own feelings and about what you want
* help other people understand what you are saying
* are clear, honest and direct
* make your point without blaming, criticizing or judging other people.

An 'I' statement:
* describes the behaviour I'm finding difficult
* says the effect it has on me
* tells the other person how I feel about it
* invites them to join me in finding a solution.

Broken record is another useful technique to make sure that you are listened to and that your message is received. 'Broken record' refers to those old vinyl discs we used to play – you may remember them or at least have heard about them. They were activated by a needle that went round a groove and when one had been damaged the needle would often skip and get stuck in a groove and keep repeating the same bit. In broken record what you do is keep repeating your point or your request until the other person recognizes and acknowledges what you are saying.

The keys to using broken record effectively are:
* being clear about what you want
* standing your ground
* not losing your temper

* making it clear that you've heard and recognized what the other person is saying to you and sympathize. Phrases to use would be 'I can see. . .', 'You say. . .', 'I realize. . .', 'That may be how it feels to you. . .'

This is how it might work:

Istelle: Darren, it's your turn to make the meal tonight. Everything you need is in the fridge.

Darren: I've got emails to do.

Istelle: I can see you have things you want to do, but I'd like you to start the meal now.

Darren: I'll do it when I've finished this.

Istelle: It's late and I'm sure you're as hungry as I am. I'd like you to do it now please while I have a bath.

Darren: You're always nagging me!

Istelle: I can see how you might feel I'm getting at you, but please, I want you to start the meal now.

Darren: God, you're just doing this assertive thing at me again and I hate it!

Istelle: That may be how it feels to you, but I'd like you to start cooking please.

Darren: Istelle, I've had a really hard day. Can't I just have a few minutes peace and then I'll do it.

Istelle: I realize you've had a rough day. Please make us a meal now.

Darren: OK, OK, I'm doing it.

Be polite, don't raise your voice or lose your temper. Persist, repeating the request and go on far longer than you might think would be comfortable. If you keep it calm and don't rise to any bait or argument, you will be surprised how many times you can simply repeat a message. If you're not getting anywhere, after as many attempts as you feel able to repeat, try one final time.

'I've asked you ten times and I'd like to ask you once more to please begin cooking our meal now.'

If you then feel you are getting nowhere or are losing your cool, break off saying:

'OK, we'll leave this for ten minutes and then we'll discuss it again.'

Go away and congratulate yourself for not having lost your temper and for having left the door open for further talk. After ten minutes, go back. You may find the other person has started doing what you requested – if so, thank them without further comment. If not, resume and continue. If you do this without reproaches, complaint or threats and without getting hooked into arguing, it isn't nagging. It's making yourself clear. The other person will get the message that you're serious, won't be deflected, drawn or incited to violence (verbal or otherwise) and will persist. Sooner or later, they are likely to co-operate.

Paying attention to what we say isn't enough. How you say it is actually even more significant. Here's an easy way to recognize the importance of how we put our ideas across. Think about the way people tell jokes or funny stories. One person can have you rolling on the floor with a joke or a story. But another person can tell exactly the same anecdote or gag with no effect whatsoever.

Varying degrees of disgust, sarcasm, scorn and anger in your voice transforms a simple statement into confrontation – angry words, slammed doors, tears. Mumbling, stumbling, using too may 'ums', 'ahs' and 'ers', peppering your speech with 'you know', 'like' and 'innit', can dilute the strength of what you want to say or even change the meaning. Using slang and the sort of short-cut references that come from having shared jokes or seen the same films and TV shows can help when talking with family, friends or close colleagues but may not work when used with people from another generation or in a formal setting. Approach your boss and say 'Umm, er, what I want to ask, if you don't mind, I mean, it's like, you know, I'd sort of like a pay rise' would have a very different result from saying 'Can we talk? I've been looking at what I've been doing for the company lately and in the light of new responsibilities and productivity I'd like us to discuss an increase in my salary'. The reverse can also be true: using very formal or elaborate language out of place can be just as unhelpful.

In relearning how to talk, you focus on your tone and pitch. If you listen to how the people you like or trust or respect talk, you can pick up tips on how you can do it too. Range and variety are important. Talking all on one level sounds monotonous and boring, and also makes you appear nervous. Listen to how you talk when you're with people with whom you feel comfortable. Your voice is likely to be warmer, more animated, with far more ups and downs and variations. Then listen to yourself when you're feeling threatened. Voices tend to go up in pitch and to flatten out when we're unsure. Pitching your voice down low, so it conveys warmth and control rather than nervousness, can make a difference not only to how others see you, but to how you see yourself. This is not about changing your accent or 'learning how to speak proper'; it's about being yourself but with self-confidence.

Practice makes perfect. Initially, practise in your mind and imagine yourself using 'I' statements or responding to other people's attempts at dominating or manipulating you. Visualize yourself behaving in a firmer manner, saying firmer things, asking firm, clear, probing questions, and presenting well-prepared facts and evidence. What you will be doing is re-conditioning yourself, gradually, from responding either with 'Yes, of course!' or 'Oh dear, it's all too much!' or 'Don't talk to me like that!' to more effective reactions.

Responses you could use might be:
* I need to think that over. I'll come back to you.
* If you want an answer now it's no. If we can talk this over and I have time to think about it, it might be different.
* Yes, I can do that, but I will need more information/time to make arrangements/some support.
* No, I can't do that.
* I'd be happy to help but not today. Tomorrow/next Thursday/next week is good.

And it isn't just the words and the tone in which we say things that adds to either our meaning or the understanding of the recipient. You also need to factor in our facial expressions and our body language. These have been shown to account for over 50 per cent of meaning in our communication.

Body language describes the way you hold yourself and it too sends messages independent of the words you are using. Five important body postures are mirroring, congruence, incongruence, closed position and open position.

Mirroring is when you find yourself copying the stance of the person with whom you are talking – crossing your legs or leaning forward when they do as if you were mirror images of each other. You may not realize you are doing it and neither may the other person, but the likely effect is that both of you will feel you are in tune with each other and on the same wavelength. If you want to reassure and give confidence to someone while you are talking, this is a good way to do it. It can also be felt by the other person to mean you are in a submissive position, following their lead and doing what they choose to do. You can consciously use mirroring to instil reassurance and confidence. Used with assertion it does not appear slavish but conveys the message that you are listening.

Congruence is when your body language and your facial expressions match the words you are using. So, if you are happy and amused you'd be smiling; if serious or even unhappy, you would be solemn.

Incongruence is when your body language and your facial expressions do not match the words you are using. You may be angry or upset but smiling. You may be making a complaint, but by avoiding eye contact and crossing your arms or huddling you send out the message that you feel vulnerable and defensive.

When you say 'I'm really upset with you' but smile as you say it, or turn away to hide or avoid eye contact, this totally undercuts your words. We often do this because we're nervous and scared of the other person's reaction, or because we feel being nice while delivering criticism or complaint will prevent conflict. But the effect is not to lower the tension or deflect an angry response, it is to absolutely sabotage what you're trying to say. If your body language, your tone and your words don't match up, it doesn't make your message any more palatable, it simply causes confusion. An important aspect of assertiveness, then, is congruency – when what you say and how you say it match.

Closed position is when you cross arms and legs, or make sure there is a barrier between you and the person you are talking to – a cushion, an article of clothing, a table. The message this body position sends is that you feel under threat. The more you entwine your limbs or huddle inwards and avoid eye contact, the more defensive you appear.

Open position is when you stand or sit upright with arms held loosely, in your lap or by your side, with your legs uncrossed. This pose sends the message that you are open and receptive, confident and secure.

Making decisions is about choosing between one course of action and another. We often find it hard to prioritize and say 'This is what I will do, that is what I will not do' because it seems so final and momentous. And of course if we've decided, we're then responsible for what happens. It feels as if when we don't decide but let it happen, we can't be held accountable. But you need to remind yourself that when you leave things to take their course, that in itself is a decision to act. You are really just as liable for a decision taken passively as you are for one you actively settle on.

It's worthwhile putting any choice to a test:

Why might I go one way or another? Are you inclined for or against because of the greater good of everyone involved? Or are you biased one way because you want to please someone, are afraid of a reaction, or are being influenced by something in your past?

How long will this decision live with me? However it feels, an argument over which programme to watch on TV is not important; you may have a passing regret if around the water cooler next day you have to say 'I didn't see it', but an hour later, it really won't matter. So don't fight over the TV remote the way you might over a decision to move house.

Who else is affected by my decision? Demanding you always get your way may have lasting effects on those around you, leading them to resent you, or spend time away, shunning you. Others always being allowed to have their own way, on the other hand, sets up a situation where you become the doormat, seething in resentment while they never have to learn to compromise or think of others. Balance up your needs against other people's – neither should always take priority.

A small decision can become a big one. Who gets the TV remote and a choice of programmes can, if it always goes one way, end up with a family split down the middle and hardly communicating. While a big one – such as what exams to take – can become less significant when you can revisit and renegotiate.

Another technique that can help in becoming assertive is that of giving and receiving feedback. Feedback means the process of giving and receiving information about behaviour in a particular situation. You can give feedback about another person's behaviour to them and then they can give you feedback on your own. You can also give feedback on your own behaviour, and listen to theirs on themselves, and then discuss your reactions with each other.

Giving and receiving feedback is useful for several reasons:

* It tells you what you are doing and how you are coming across to others. You can learn from this to amend and change your behaviour if necessary.

* It can give you an insight into how you behave. Other people can often see aspects of us which we cannot see ourselves. We can particularly be blinded by a culture which tends to put people down, and teaches us to put ourselves down. If your head is full of self-critical messages, such as 'I can't really do that', 'Nobody will listen to me', 'What I think doesn't matter' you may miss what you are doing right – which someone else can see.

* Very often, it is easier to see the special qualities and uniqueness of others than it is to see your own. Exchanging feedback means you can help someone else by speaking out about their strengths, and they can do the same for you.

When giving and receiving feedback it's often useful to use these two questions:

* What did I/they do well?
* What could I/they do differently?

It is far more effective to think about what you could have done differently than what you think you might have done wrong. We tend to be self-critical and focus on our mistakes, which can actually lock you into a self-fulfilling cycle; you think about what you did wrong and so keep repeating it, unable to see another option. That doesn't help when you are usually doing the best you can and what you need is a boost to learn from what happens and take it a step further. So, start by being reminded of how well you did, by someone else and yourself. Once you have heard this and taken it in, it is much more likely that you will be able to hear and use the comments about how you might change.

Feedback should always be:

Specific. Rather than being told 'you are terrific', it is good to hear exactly what you did or said, or how you were, that made you so effective. 'You were so friendly and kind with that salesperson – it really made him go the extra mile for us.'

Descriptive. The more detail that you can say in answer to what you thought someone did well or could have done differently, the more resource of information the recipient has to draw on and learn from. It is not helpful to get into judgemental, evaluative and critical comments. 'You'd washed up the cups and put them away. You left the wet drying up cloth on the table.'

Directed towards behaviour that can change. So, comments on someone's height, for example, which is not something that can be changed, are not helpful. But saying 'When you stand up straight you present an imposing figure – I feel I should look up to you' may help someone who is shy about their height and tends to hunch up.

Provided straight after the given behaviour. Feedback has most impact when you can link it with what you did or said. So it's best when it's fresh in your mind.

For many of us, it's in the family that we feel most hard done by and in the family where we are most in need of assertiveness skills. Yet while we may see the sense and take the step of learning how to stand up for ourselves in work or in public, it's often in the family where we feel awkward at making changes. Partly that's because we fear being ridiculed the most. When I began using these skills, having learned them while training to be a Relate counsellor, my stepson would cry 'Don't you try those counsellor tricks on me!' and my husband would respond to any thanks or appreciation by saying 'That sounds so odd! You don't have to thank me!' Family can have a way of being far more personally critical and even abusive than friends, colleagues or strangers. Since, however, it is the family that is often the breeding ground for bad habits, it's often the best place to start, and the most important place to learn, practise and perfect those skills. We'll look in more detail at how your changes can affect others in a later chapter, but for now it's worth laying down some ground rules for dealing with children and partners, parents and in-laws. You will need to:

Model what you want. If you want your family to be assertive rather than doormats or aggressors, you need to model it to them. You need to walk the talk, and that sometimes means getting tough with them. It means gaining the skills and going through the techniques and strategies, just as you are doing or learning how to do with anyone and anywhere else. You need to use 'I' messages, broken record and learn not to pull punches or lessen their impact. I might have got 'Don't you try those counsellor tricks on me!' and 'That sounds so odd! You don't have to thank me!' at first. Far more quickly than I had expected, I got 'Oh. Alright. Fine!' and 'Hey – I see what you mean, it does sound nice to be thanked!' And not too much longer after that, I began to see all those techniques coming back at me – people being clear, saying what they wanted and how they felt, and showing appreciation.

Be side by side rather than in opposition. In several recent reports on child happiness, one issue that was highlighted was how often children were able to say their parents talked with them. In the UK and USA, which both had astoundingly bad scores, children said the most frequent interaction between parent and child was for the parent to be criticizing and telling them off. In countries such as Norway and the Netherlands, which came out very well for childhood happiness, children said their parents would often 'just chat' and show an interest. One way of looking at it is to consider whether you see yourself side by side with, or in opposition to, your children. Are you walking up the hill with them, holding hands and chatting happily? Or are you dragging them along or driving them ahead of you? The assertive model is side by side. So is the happy one! In the end, it's far more important that you and your family enjoy each other's company than the place runs on clockwork. The dust comes back tomorrow – an alienated child or spouse may not.

Reinforce good behaviour, not bad. It's important to zero in on the behaviour you want not the behaviour you don't. This has the effect of reinforcing, or encouraging the repetition of, good behaviour while ignoring the bad. People hear what you say, not what you leave unsaid. And they usually want to be noticed and acknowledged. If children only ever get attention when you tell them off, however unpleasant the process of being told off is, it's better than no attention at all. So when you pick up on the things you don't want and repeat them, instead of putting them off you actually encourage them to continue.

Modelling what you want and being clear about what you would like pays off. Pay attention when they do something that pleases you and thank them for it rather than waiting for something that upsets you and drawing attention to it. Say what you want not what you don't want.

One area in which many people find it difficult to be assertive is with their own parents. Parents knew you when you were a baby, a toddler, a child and a teenager. They watched you grow up and leave home but for many of them, that separation during the teenage years and that departure is hard to accept. It's as if they still see you as you were many years before – a child, needing their support and unable to cope on your own. When parents offer advice or help, it often grates. Sometimes this is because of how they do it and why they do it – as if they were still the adults and you the child. But sometimes, advice and suggestions you'd happily accept from a friend drive you into a rage when they come from a parent.

It's not their manner or expectation which is at fault but your sensitivity to where it comes from.

You shouldn't have to tolerate behaviour from a relative that you wouldn't tolerate from a colleague, a friend or acquaintance. However, family are your support network; sometimes you have to accept that their behaviour may be undesirable and they may not see any reason to change. You can't change other people, you can only change yourself. But behaving differently yourself can have some powerful effects.

When parents visit or we go home to see them – at family festivals or at weekends – it's easy to fall back into familiar patterns of behaviour, with them and with siblings. Parents may treat their children as if they were, or should be, living at home again, to the bafflement and often fury of their partners. There may be criticism of the state of clothes, of whether you're eating enough or doing well enough, or of your children. Or parents may tell stories or conduct conversations in ways that say 'We were here first and this is where you have your primary loyalty' and that exclude the new people in their adult children's lives.

You may also find that when you see siblings, you all drop back into feeling, and behaving, the way you did when you were young and at home. Grown men and women may squabble, argue and fight over petty things. What you're actually doing is reviving quarrels from years ago – fighting over who gets the most attention, who are favourites, who comes first in your parents' eyes.

Being assertive on family visits requires some preparation. If you find them hard, ask yourself these questions:

What triggers set me off?

Is it a tone of voice, a way of speaking to you, those family stories retold and retold? Sit down and think about the last time you were with them and put your finger on exactly what it was that upset you. Write them down.

What does it remind me of?

Then ask yourself – where does that particular behaviour take you? Does it remind you generally of being a child again or of specific incidents? What's the hook – how does it pull you back to the past? List these, too.

How do I feel when I find it difficult?

And most important of all, when you've answered the previous two questions, explore how it makes you feel. Angry? Jealous? Humiliated? Obligated? Under pressure to fulfil certain expectations? Do you feel you've been a disappointment or that you now have to come up to certain standards?

Once you can analyse what happens and why, you can plan in advance. Don't forget that when people seem to have power over you, it's only because you hand the power to them. You can claim it back. Seeing triggers and anticipating them means when they pop up, you can say 'Oh yes – the old family story which tells me I'm four years old again.' Forewarned is forearmed. These things have so much power because they operate under the level of conscious thought. Once you've brought them out into the open they lose much of their force. Once you know this behaviour hooks you back into feelings that properly belong in your past, you can pack them off there rather than allowing them to replay again. You can say 'Oh yes, I used to feel really angry/jealous/humiliated. But that was then. Now is now.'

7

accepting
and giving
criticism

Fear of being criticized can be a major factor holding you back from becoming assertive. But knowing how to receive, and indeed give, criticism gracefully and effectively are key skills to becoming assertive. Discerning the motives behind your giving criticism, and behind the criticism levelled at you, can help you manage it. Criticism can be intended as a support and help or to undermine. Understanding what lies behind it can often help you extract what might be useful and ignore what might be destructive and unhelpful. Knowing when and how to ignore it, laugh at it or address the underlying issue of the critic can help you address criticism in a positive way. We'll explore the skill of 'fogging' where you defuse the power of unfair or maliciously intended criticism by robbing your critic's words of their destructive power, and look at knowing how to learn from mistakes and move on, a vital aspect of assertiveness.

Knowing how to both accept and give criticism in a positive way is key to being assertive. It sometimes seems as if we're surrounded by criticism – 'everyone's a critic', as they say. The fear of criticism is what puts many people off seeking to assert themselves. Nobody likes being held up and torn down unfairly. But we sometimes fear and avoid what can be seen as fair criticism even more. It's the anxiety about putting ourselves in the firing line and both attracting and having to deal with rigorous examination that can make us hold back. So why do we all find criticism hard to accept? How can we take valid criticism on board and how do we deal with it? What should we do when judgements are being made and we don't feel they are valid? And how should we ourselves deliver criticism so it is helpful?

The motives of the person offering it, and their actual intention, can be significant. However, whether criticism helps or not isn't always about whether it was intended as a help or a hindrance. It depends on the attitude of the person on the receiving end, and what they take from it. Someone can give you a positive, thoughtful assessment with the very best intentions and if you are feeling defensive it can simply feel like an attack. On the other hand, someone can be judgemental and disparaging with the main intention of hurting your feelings, and if you are self-confident and know your worth, you can actually take something from it.

When receiving criticism, it's worthwhile taking a moment to work out the probable intention of the critic. This can help you because sometimes you need to dive under their words or behaviour. If you can determine they wanted to undermine you rather than help you, you may need to choose to sidestep what has been said. Being assertive often means knowing when you don't have to take on board something that has been offered to you.

But even if the intention was hurtful, you still may recover something useful from what is being said. You could take much of what is offered with some scepticism, but there may be some truth in it and that might be useful.

Criticism offered with the intention of being helpful should always be considered, even if you don't like what you hear.

You may still decide to reject what is being said, but at least it's important to think about what is being offered. Friends, family or colleagues who take the risk of being shot as the messenger by telling you something unwelcome may well have a message you need to listen to.

When offering criticism, consider why you are giving it. Are you upset or angry, and wanting to make that plain? Do you want to cut the person down to size? Do you want to make yourself or your achievements look better by giving them doubts or reducing theirs? Or is your motive to help them do better, to boost their confidence and their abilities? Sometimes the painful truth is that we have destructive and negative reasons for offering what we do, and we need to consider and examine these before saying anything. If you're angry or upset, it's better to say so rather than using roundabout ways of delivering a reproof. It doesn't get to the heart of the problem if you hand out a stinging attack on someone's work or their leaving the bathroom in a mess, when what is really bothering you is that they didn't consult you, or are taking you for granted – or haven't said they love you in a week! And it won't help if you attack them personally rather than focusing on what it is they did to upset you.

Even destructive criticism that is meant to undermine can be turned to an advantage. You need, however, to ask yourself this question because what often at first seems hurtful and difficult is actually intended to help. A significant aspect to look at is whether it's your behaviour that is being held up for examination, or you. Helpful criticism always highlights behaviour, not people. When someone says, for instance, 'You're lazy', 'You're nasty' or 'You're selfish', it is personal – the individual is being attacked, and labelled. When you're told 'You are....', where can you go? It's hard to move forward when you're stuck with being whatever it is that has upset the person saying this. When, instead, what is pointed to is a particular bit of behaviour – and the more specific the better – we can address that. So, instead of 'You're lazy', what might be said is 'I asked you to take out the rubbish and you didn't – please do it now.' Instead of 'You're nasty', what might be said is 'When you said that you hurt my feelings.' Instead of 'You're selfish', what might be said is 'It upset me that you made that arrangement without consulting with me first.' When we address the behaviour rather than the person, we begin to move towards a solution.

Think about what you say and how you say it. Don't forget, your words only tell a fraction of the story. Whether you make eye contact, your stance, the tone and level of your voice all contribute to making both giving and receiving criticism a positive experience.

In some cases, criticism is valid: they're right. How do you react assertively to criticism? You accept it. But you do so cheerfully, with a desire to do better in the future, and no intention of letting it make you feel bad about yourself or blame yourself. You don't take it personally, even if there was a personal element.

So if a friend or work colleague complains you're late arriving, say 'Yes, you're right. I need to organize my time better.' Don't make excuses and certainly don't lie to cover yourself. Even if you feel it wasn't your fault – a late train, someone at home distracting you – still take the responsibility. After all, the chances are with more thought or foresight you could have been on time. So own it, and change your behaviour if you want to, or don't change if you don't want to – but either way, don't beat yourself up or let it lead to an argument just because you've been criticized.

Another way of taking responsibility is simply owning up to your mistakes before anyone says anything. Again, you turn up late and the first thing you say is 'I'm late – sorry! My fault and I will do better from now on.' By acknowledging the problem and accepting responsibility for the situation, you take back control.

Dealing positively with criticism requires you to listen, acknowledge, assess and come up with answers. If what has been said feels difficult and painful to take on board, ask for a time to assess the situation – to cool down and collect your thoughts. Don't let yourself be hustled into reacting immediately if you need this time. You're not using it to look for a defence or a way out of the situation – you're looking for a way of managing what has been said in the best possible manner. If an immediate reply is demanded, a useful thing to say is 'It's a no if you want an answer at once; a probable yes if you can give me some time to think.'

Often if you're struggling with criticism it helps to ask for elaboration or rephrasing. If criticism is given indirectly, ask for a direct statement. You can't deal head on with games-playing, you can with honesty. Opening up the situation may help you see a solution. The more specific it is, the better for all of you. You, to see what you might be able to do to improve things. Them, to perhaps see what they saw as a problem isn't quite as bad as they thought. And for both of you, to focus your minds on moving on rather than being stuck. The most important tip for handling criticism is to accept responsibility. That might mean accepting you made a mistake or it might mean your carrying the buck for someone else, because the ultimate accountability was yours. Whatever, sometimes that is all you can do and all that is required.

Of course, if you don't agree, or partially agree, say so and why. This is why asking for the criticism to be specific is so important. Simply saying 'I don't agree' can sound defensive and inauthentic. You're simply refusing to examine what has been said or to entertain the sentiments being offered. But if you have been told 'You did such and such' or 'You failed to do so and so' and you can give specific examples to contradict, or to modify what has been suggested, you can show that you are willing to change if change is what is required.

How do you manage when you realize the other person isn't so much criticizing you as putting you down with the sole motive to depress and upset you and to take control of the situation? When someone puts you down, a natural response is to want to get your own back or to defend yourself. Defending yourself usually has a negative impact on both you and the other person. This often escalates into conflict – arguments, backbiting and feuds.

Put-downs hook you into feeling insecure and low in self-worth. But they're really about the insecurity and low self-worth of the person doing it to you. They're relying on you responding in a way that boosts their ego and sense of power and control. When you react, especially by going on the defensive, you do just that. Put-downs rely on a reaction from you.

When dealing with a put-down you can:

* Ignore it. This is about others trying to make themselves feel better at your expense. So let the remark float over your head. They're likely to stop when you do not give them the satisfaction of a reaction.
* Laugh at it. Make a joke that deflects and defuses the situation.
* Address the underlying need – that of the other person's need to feel better. Ask them if there is anything with which you can help, encourage and support them.

One technique that often proves useful when faced with unfair criticism, or criticism that has a main aim of getting at you, is fogging. Fogging is a strategy that can defuse the power of criticism to hurt or depress you. It's a helpful approach when what you're being offered is negative and unfair. Fogging is so named because instead of going head to head in conflict, you offer no apparent resistance. If you stand your ground someone can attack you. If you turn and run, they can pursue you. But if you imagine a bank of fog blowing up and enveloping both of you, you can see your critic can get lost. And when you're lost in a fog, there's no point fighting it or shouting at it; it simply melts away and so resists your attempts at intimidation or influence. What you do with fogging is to agree, deflect, and remain calm and reasonable. You do not allow yourself to be provoked or upset by what is being said. You consider what is said, agree with whatever may be fair and useful and turn the criticism around. Fogging requires some self-control, but it can be enormously effective.

So, for instance, if your teenager turns up their nose at your spaghetti bolognaise, saying 'Yuck, I'm not eating that, it's horrible!', you could be hurt by the criticism or angry at the rejection. Or, you could recognize that all teenagers have to rebel and needle their parents and you might say 'Oh, I am sorry you don't like it. There's bread in the bin, and I'm sure we can share yours out between us or maybe the cat would like it. . .'

The point of fogging is that it robs your critic's words of their destructive power. You may find it hard at first because it feels as if you're backing down and giving in. But your refusal to become upset or angry in the face of criticism is the strongest defence of all. By remaining calm, you're denying your critic the satisfaction of seeing you upset or browbeaten and of losing control and having your power taken away. If what is at the root of their behaviour is an attempt to bully you, and it doesn't succeed, your critic is likely to back off. Like that fog, you just melt away before them, leaving them hitting out at the mist.

Useful phrases to use when fogging are: 'That could be true', 'I see what you mean', 'I'm sorry you feel that way. . .', 'You may be right' and 'You have a point there.' What you hold firm to while fogging is the recognition that whatever the criticism, justified or not, you will learn from what is being said but you will not give up your power or control or your good self-image of yourself.

An important aspect of assertiveness is the ability to learn from mistakes, and then move on. When we're being passive, passive-aggressive or aggressive we dwell, deny or nag about these. We criticize others unfairly, trying to shift responsibility or blame, and we go into avoidance when someone criticizes us. You dwell and obsess about the smallest issue, when you can't set it aside. The trick is to accept and encompass, learn and then move forward. You can't be perfect; everyone makes mistakes and that's OK. Accepting that fact is really important because when you believe that perfection exists and you have to aspire to it, you can find yourself in trouble. You may stop trying and fall back, despondent and believing you can never achieve anything. Or you become particularly and unrealistically critical of others, demanding standards that no one can achieve. Assertiveness demands that you go on pushing boundaries and taking risks, even if it leads to your making more mistakes.

accepting
and giving
compliments

While most of us would recognize that giving and accepting criticism are difficult issues but important when learning how to be assertive, we may not realize how equally vital it is to be able to offer and accept a compliment. Giving and accepting compliments relates to how people value themselves and others. Knowing your own value and recognizing and acknowledging that of other people is an important aspect of assertiveness and strategies such as having a Self-Worth Wall in your home can help. Many of us when given a compliment will refuse it, trivialize, or undermine it, so we shall explore how and why to accept compliments. To be effective compliments need to be small, simple, spontaneous and specific. They also benefit enormously from being given as descriptive praise, and we'll look at why that is and how to do it.

You probably agree that accepting and giving criticism would be a difficult issue for most of us. We fear being judged and often do our utmost to avoid it. How we deal with criticism is clearly an important part of learning to be assertive, and it's easy to realize that. What we may not recognize is that how we deal with compliments, both the accepting and the giving of them, is actually equally important and significant.

Giving and accepting compliments is vital to being assertive for one important reason: they relate to how we value ourselves, and how we value others. Value is an important concept when dealing with assertiveness. We can assert ourselves when we recognize our own value – that we are worthwhile, that we deserve to be respected and that we respect ourselves, and those around us. And indeed, we can allow other people to be assertive without reverting to being passive, passive-aggressive or aggressive with them when we can recognize their value too, and see it as complementary to ours, not in competition. Not having been valued in childhood is often the reason why people are unassertive and have low self-esteem and low self-confidence. Part of learning to assert ourselves is learning also to value ourselves.

So how we accept and give compliments is as relevant to assertiveness as is accepting and giving criticism. And how do we generally deal with compliments? In our culture, on the whole, badly!

Think of the last time someone paid you a compliment. Did you:

Refuse it. When someone compliments us, we often push them away, snubbing them and insisting that we don't want to accept what they say. We laugh, flap our hands and say something along the lines of 'Please don't make a fuss!'

Trivialize it. Compliments are often met with a denial. When, for instance, someone remarks on what an attractive outfit you are wearing, you may respond 'What, this old thing?'

Undermine it. When someone remarks on what a good job you have done, it's frequently met with 'Oh no, it was nothing, really.'

We refuse, trivialize or undermine compliments for several reasons. It might be because:

We're embarrassed. If we're struggling with issues of self-esteem and confidence, we may not like to be in the spotlight. Accepting a compliment may feel like making yourself vulnerable – and putting yourself in the position of having to come up with the goods again!

We feel we don't deserve them. Lacking the self-esteem to accept you deserve a compliment may be the most important reason we refuse them.

We feel we should be modest. Decades of being told 'Don't be boastful', 'Don't get above yourself' or 'You're no one special' often leaves us with the conviction that we shouldn't seek or accept compliments, because doing so is bad manners.

Perhaps the last generation, or the one before that, appreciates such conduct. But the reality is that when you give a compliment and it is refused, trivialized or undermined, you don't admire this behaviour. Instead, you feel:

Rebuffed. You offered a gift or what you knew was earned and had it thrown back in your face.

Insulted. You made a judgement and expressed it, and had the other person in effect tell you your judgement was wrong.

Unimpressed. Instead of feeling the person refusing the compliment was being appropriately modest, we're more likely to think they were being inappropriately self-effacing.

It isn't being arrogant or selfish, nor does it mean you take anything away from anyone else to gracefully say 'Thank you!' when someone says 'Well done' or 'I like that'. Phrases you might find helpful are:

'Thank you!'
'I'm glad you like it.'
'I'm pleased you enjoyed it.'
'I appreciate your saying that.'
'That's very kind of you.'

If you feel other people contributed you can also say:

'I'll pass on your compliment to the rest of them.'
'I'm sure everyone will be glad to hear that.'

When accepting compliments, don't let your body language or tone undercut what you are saying. Make eye contact, smile and use open gestures to reinforce your message that you hear what is being said, accept it and acknowledge it.

Most importantly, take the compliment away, think about it and use it. If self-esteem, self-worth and self-confidence are issues for you, compliments are part of your toolbox to raise them.

One thing you should have in your home is a Self-Worth Wall. Every home should have one. Choose somewhere in your home that you see every day. It could be in the hallway or in the kitchen. Use the whole wall, or put up a notice board. This is where you and anyone else in your home is going to blow their own trumpet. Make a note of any and all achievements. You could stick up certificates or letters, or emails. When someone pays you a compliment face to face or on the phone or by text, make a note of it and pin it here, so you can see it and be reminded of it, and so can everyone else. 'John told me I did a really good job of that project today!', 'Sarah said I looked especially nice in my new dress.' Encourage your whole family to do this for themselves; it's a good idea for all of you to add little notes and anything else that catches your fancy to pass on a message of support and appreciation.

You do need to raise your self-esteem and self-confidence, and increase your appreciation of your own worth in order to be assertive. Which is why, as well as being able to recognize and accept compliments, you need to understand that the person you most need to approve of you is yourself. You are the ultimate judge of your own behaviour. When you see that and can respect yourself, other people's compliments become a pleasure to hear. But they are not what you need to chase after or seek. You know what you deserve and are worth already. Being reliant on what other people think of you is the enemy of assertiveness. It's nice and it's pleasant to hear what they say and know what they think. But it's not the be-all and end-all.

How should you raise your own self-esteem? The Self-Worth Wall is an excellent strategy. What would work in your life?

A 'stroke' is any action that tells someone you're happy to see them, pleased to be with them and glad about something they might have done. Strokes may be verbal, when you say 'Thank you' or 'I liked that'. They can also be actions, such as making someone a cup of coffee or giving them a hug. When we give strokes it 'models' behaviour – lets people see how nice it is and how to do it. Give strokes and you soon find them coming back at you. We can, and should, also give ourselves strokes – help yourself to an apple, settle down with a magazine, book or TV programme knowing it's right and proper and deserved that you have this time to yourself, doing what you want.

Reward yourself, regularly. You make small gains and small victories all the time and the more you recognize that, the higher your esteem will be – and the better you will perform. Pats on the back from other people are welcome but one from yourself is actually just as, if not more, valuable. Rewards can be small – a glass of wine with dinner, a few moments online emailing friends – or large – deciding you will go on that special holiday you've always dreamed about this year. But the act of rewarding yourself – of recognizing you deserve a treat because you deserve recognition – is the key thing.

The rule for giving compliments is to use the four Ss – Small, Simple, Spontaneous and Specific.

Small. What you say or how you recognize merit need not be elaborate or extensive. The fact of saying or doing it is more important than the reward. So, just saying 'Thanks!' or 'Bravo!' or offering a biscuit with that cup of coffee is sufficient to get over the message that you noticed and think they deserve a pat on the back. You should never hold back from giving small and frequent compliments and affirmations of people's worth and ability – that's nice, that's pretty, that was well done.

Simple. A single daffodil picked from your own garden when given with affection or respect – or both! – as a way of recognizing merit is worth any hand-tied bouquet if you mean it. You should never feel your offering is too simple or not elaborate enough.

Spontaneous. Sometimes, measured and thought out praise has great worth, showing you've carefully considered what you want to say. But often there is no substitute for an instant reaction that says 'I just had to speak up at once!' People often bite their lip, feeling a compliment or comment would be out of place or inappropriate and by the time they realize it would be welcome, the moment feels as if it has passed. You should always speak up or act with that touch on the arm or hug when it strikes you.

Specific. Saying 'Well done!' or 'Bravo' or 'You did fine!' can sometimes be helpful, but being specific can be the best way of raising self-esteem. General praise can give a warm glow but often we're not sure exactly what it was for – what behaviour of ours the person passing the compliment actually appreciated. When you are specific, you tell the person exactly what it was you liked. Not only do they know where they stand with you, they also have every incentive to repeat it. 'You hung up the towels in the bathroom. Thank you!'; 'That casserole you made was delicious!'; 'You did that job on time, and did it well – bravo.'

Descriptive praise is an excellent strategy for giving specific compliments. When we're pleased with someone, we often tell them that they are 'good' or say 'well done'. This is great, but often it doesn't actually tell the person what they've done, why we like it and what we would like them to continue doing. It tells them about us, that *we* are happy, but it doesn't tell them about *them*, that they are capable and competent. Descriptive praise does exactly this. So, when you come home and find your teenager has washed up after having a snack and fed the cat, instead of 'Aren't you good!' say 'You fed the cat and washed up. You cleared the deck so now I can get on with preparing a meal. That was really helpful. Thank you!' Instead of thinking 'Yeah, well, whatever. . . but what did I do?' the teenager thinks 'Yeah! I'm really helpful! I can do that!' and has every incentive to repeat the behaviour, and a clear idea of what you appreciate. Giving descriptive praise sounds a bit odd at first – itemizing exactly what has been done feels so awkward. Start doing it and you'll soon realize how easy it is, and how very effective. 'You did all the washing up before I came home. Thank you!'; 'You stayed by me when we went to the supermarket and helped me fill the trolley. Thank you!'; 'You wrote that report and included all the elements we'd discussed. Thank you!'

9

saying no

Saying no is without a doubt one of the most difficult issues when learning to be assertive. It's felt to be rude, selfish and unreasonable. It's a vital skill and one that takes practice. We look at learning a few home truths – you have the right to say no, it's neither rude nor unfair and doing so appropriately is likely to gain you self-respect and the respect of others. Strategies for refusing other people's requests gracefully will be discussed such as pre-empting and being direct and honest. You'll be encouraged to take your time, to watch your stance and body language and what you say, and to pay attention to your own feelings. We'll also look at resisting 'the hook' and accepting feeling guilty when you first start thinking of yourself and saying no to other people's requests. Saying no is important because if you only ever say yes, your 'yes' has far less value to others than when it is sparing and considered.

One of the most difficult areas for most unassertive people is being able to say no. If you're struggling with being submissive or passive, the likelihood is that you say yes all the time – yes to helping people out, yes to taking on other people's responsibilities as your own, yes to doing far too much.

If you find yourself reverting to aggressive or passive-aggressive modes when faced with calls on your time you may indeed be able to say no. But in doing so, you may alienate and upset people either by being abrupt or hostile, or by complaining and grumbling. The assertive option is to be able to refuse, but to do so leaving everyone feeling OK about it. That takes skill and practice. So where do you start? You begin by settling a few home truths in your own mind:

* You have the right to say no.
* Just because someone asks, doesn't mean you have to do.
* You're being neither rude nor unfair to refuse.
* If you never say no what is your yes worth?
* You'll respect and like yourself more if you stand up for yourself.
* Other people will respect and like you more if you stand up for yourself.

So how do you do it?

Pre-empt if possible. If you know someone is bearing down on you, ready to ask a favour; if you know when the phone goes it's going to be that friend or relative, expecting you to drop everything for them, get in first. Say 'Before we go on, can I just say I'm really busy today and I'm not going to be able to help you out.' Be pleasant but firm. And use broken record if they insist. You can always say 'I'm going to have to interrupt you and go. Lovely to see/speak with you. Goodbye!'

You can give a simple 'No'. You don't owe them an explanation. You may give reasons but certainly not excuses. Unless you're in the Forces or another emergency occupation, you're not in a situation where someone in authority can tell you what to do and it's a sacking offence if you refuse. You don't need to carry an assumption of having to do something over into your private life. You might choose to add:

* I would prefer not to, thank you.
* I'm not willing to, thank you
* I don't want to, thank you.

If you might say yes but on your terms, check out the request and don't respond immediately. Ask for more information and clarification about what is wanted, when, where and for how long. In order to keep control of the situation you might like to say 'If you want an immediate answer it's no. If you give me time to think about it, it might be yes.'

Being direct and honest works. White lies, excuses or playing for time tend to end up in the worst of all worlds. You'll either have to work increasingly and desperately hard at avoiding what or whoever it was, and still end up doing it, or upset and alienate them and make yourself feel bad. If you are not direct, it can lead to several problems:

* People continue to ask you to do things because you've not said 'No', only 'Not at the moment'.
* You feel resentful, angry and guilty.
* You have to keep track of your excuses and white lies.
* People begin to feel you are avoiding or stringing them along.

On the other hand, a direct 'No' has many benefits:
* It saves time – if you can't or don't want to do it, the request ends there.
* Everyone knows exactly where they stand.
* You can negotiate a better deal for you if you do choose to help – a win/win solution for everyone.
* You all feel better – you don't feel resentful and other people don't have to find you've lied to them.

13 tips for saying no

Recognize you have the same rights as everyone else. Your time, your choices, your wishes and your well-being are every bit as important as theirs. They may feel their wish for you to do what they want is paramount. It isn't. You matter too.

Take your time. If the other person or persons try to hurry you into a decision, take your time. If you know someone is going to ask or expect you to do something you don't want to do, spend some time before seeing them thinking it over. What might they ask? What would you like to do, what would you not want to do? Concentrate on a positive outcome for you both – and remember that giving in may not be as positive for them as they may think. Be clear about what you want to say or achieve by the conversation or encounter. If you don't feel ready, politely but firmly suggest it be undertaken at a later time or date.

Watch your stance. If they're sitting, sit down with them. If they're standing, stand up too. If it's a child, or someone in a wheelchair, crouch down. Make eye contact and make sure the person is connecting to you and the conversation by saying their name and if appropriate, touching a hand, arm or leg.

Watch your body language. You don't want to be defensive, nor do you want to be saying you'll do as they ask with the way you appear. Crossing arms, hunching over, turning away all say you're defensive. Smiling while trying to refuse a request gives the answer yes, whatever your words are saying. Turning towards the other person, with your hands in your lap or your arms by side in a relaxed position says you're listening. 'Mirroring' – having the same stance in reverse of the person you're talking to – can send the message that you're on the same wavelength. Crowding someone by coming into their personal space is aggressive; standing your ground and allowing someone their space is assertive.

Watch what you say. You don't need to explain yourself. Giving elaborate excuses for why you are not going to do something undercuts your refusal. It tells the other person you think you owe them something. That gives them the opening they need – all they need to do is overcome your excuses by finding another time or place or favour and you'll then say yes.

Watch your feelings and how they are being revealed when you do talk with someone asking you to do something you don't want to do. Clenched fists? Gritted teeth? Are you hunching over, crossing arms, turning away – all signs that you feel vulnerable? If you can see them so can the other person. Take a deep breath and relax, or politely but firmly say you'll stop now and resume at another time.

Resist the hook. People who know you also know how to hook you in by playing on your sense of responsibility or guilt. Every time you say yes when you should have said no, their behaviour is reinforced – that is, they know it works and will do it again. Saying no now sets the scene for being able to say no afterwards. Say yes now and you'll keep on saying it.

Put up with the guilt. When you begin to say no you'll probably feel guilty: you should have said yes, what will they think of you, it won't take a moment. . . Grit your teeth and accept it. It's only the weight of all those years of being made to feel you should put yourself out speaking. In time, you'll realize you don't have to feel that way at all, and you won't.

Consider the outcome. What could they do if you did say no? And if you were away or ill and couldn't do what is being asked of you, what would they do? What is the worst thing that might happen if you say 'no'? How likely is that to happen?

Start small and gain experience. Say no to something small and unimportant, just to be able to know the sky doesn't fall when you do. Remind yourself of that when you need to say no to something big.

Recognize it takes time. It took years to make you someone who always said yes. It may take months to become someone who can say no when it's appropriate. Celebrate your triumphs, understand your small setbacks and continue the process. It's hard work but it will be worthwhile.

Sometimes, say yes. Once you say no to the things that aren't your responsibility or you can't take on or simply choose not to do, you will learn how to discriminate. Then, you can say yes to things you have the time and inclination to take on or simply choose to do. Once you can say no and are known for it, your yes will be valued all the more. Saying yes all the time doesn't make you valued or liked, it makes you a doormat. Choosing when you will or won't makes you worthwhile.

Don't make it personal. By your words, manner and behaviour make it clear that this isn't about them, it's about you. You aren't saying no because you don't love them, don't like them, don't want to be with them or help them. You're saying no because it doesn't suit you, you don't choose to do it. . . and that's that.

10

changing others by changing yourself

When we look at becoming assertive, we often do it because we want other people in our lives to behave differently – to listen to us, not to push us around. It can be disappointing to realize you can only change yourself – you cannot seek to change other people. But once you embark on the journey of altering your own beliefs and your own behaviour you may well find it makes a difference to how others treat you. While you are only responsible for yourself, your own feelings and your own needs, a change in your beliefs and behaviour cannot help but affect those around you.

It's like being on a seesaw or teeter totter. If you both stand at either end you're balanced. If you want to move forward you can ask, demand and scream at the other person to move. If they decide not to, you can't make them. But if you begin to inch forward, they have to move too . . . or fall off.

Because of the way we have evolved, we incline towards fight or flight. Both have survival implications in a more primitive time. But in a world where we increasingly find the best survival tactic is co-operation, where we protect our own and other people's interests together instead of seeking to dominate and overcome, assertive behaviour is important.

Becoming more assertive means inevitably that you impact on those around you. The people whose behaviour led to your wanting to learn how to assert yourself in the first place – family or friends, work colleagues or people you encounter in public – will react to the new you. Their response may be welcoming and positive. With your new found self-esteem and confidence, recognizing how much this benefits you, you may want to spread the advantages around to those you know. Or, of course, they may react with surprise or even hostility.

Passing on what you have learned can help those around you to deal with your assertiveness, and makes life a lot easier for you. It can also help them become more assertive themselves. There is, however, a catch. The reality is that you cannot change other people. You may want to do so, and hope that by demanding it or wishing it, they will see the sense of what you are asking and do as you ask. It doesn't happen that way. You can't force behaviour change on other people. Their behaviour and their beliefs are their responsibility, not yours. But by being assertive yourself you can show them how assertive behaviour is a helpful model to follow.

We often wish we could change the people with whom we have conflict or who intimidate us. If only they would change, we think, we'd be all right. We wouldn't have to work at being assertive and our troubles would be over. It's other people who seem to be the problem – why can't they be different?

There are several problems with this approach. One is that by seeking to change other people, we make them accountable, and thus in control, for how we feel and how we act. That may not be the real issue. It may be our approach that needs to alter. And whether it is us or them at the root of it, we should always accept that it is we who are responsible for our own feelings and actions. Since we can never bank on someone else changing for our convenience, it's not an effective way of seeking to make things better.

It might feel comfortable and handy to blame someone else for the situation or our emotions. That's a very human way of doing it. But isn't it actually better to take charge? If you accept it might be down to you, you are then in control of turning it all around. Instead of being a victim, you're in control. When it comes down to it, it doesn't really matter whether other people or you are to blame, what matters is that it improves. And since you can get on with streamlining and improving on your own, without having to persuade or wait for others to be ready, taking responsibility for yourself and your changes is simply so effective.

For you to really get the best out of an encounter, you and the other person both should be acting assertively. If the other person is being aggressive, they won't be listening to your views or needs; being submissive, they won't be expressing their views; and being passive-aggressive, they may be avoiding any real dialogue.

By encouraging them to listen, to express their views or by engaging them in the discussion, you not only continue to be assertive yourself, you help them to move out of their dysfunctional behaviour and join you in being effective and co-operative.

What you can do is:
* explain what you want and invite them to do the same
* put forward potential solutions or ideas and invite them to do the same
* you may need also to point out the consequence of each set of actions, which of course includes the choice of doing none of the actions discussed
* you both assess the idea to see if it meets both your needs; if not, brainstorm other ideas
* if you exhaust all ideas, agree how you will both compromise to find a solution that partly satisfies both of you
* choose a solution that meets both sets of needs.

It is your responsibility to:
* resist giving in to the other person's needs, which would be being unassertive
* take account of the other person's needs, because ignoring them would be being aggressive
* refuse to go silent or withdraw, which would be being passive-aggressive.

It is not your responsibility to:
* put the other person's needs above yours
* take on the job of looking after their needs
* feel that if they can't 'get it' it's your fault.

It probably goes without saying that you'll want to use your newly honed assertiveness skills in dealing with any children you have. Family conflict, after all, is often the most keenly felt incentive for seeking such skills. What you may not have immediately recognized is that helping your children be assertive themselves may be one of the best tactics to solve such difficulties.

When you help children be self-confident and assertive and to manage their own problems in dealing with other people as well as with you, often see a marked reduction in family arguments. Since assertiveness is not about trying to dominate others but to resist those who seek to dominate and manipulate you, teaching it to children does not encourage them be aggressive, loud or bullying. By giving them the skills to resist, of course, it does mean you will have to keep on your toes; you may not be able to dominate them anymore. You will, however, be able to draw boundaries and insist on necessary rules being kept. But you'll do it by proving a good model and asking them to buy into those rules rather than simply throwing your weight around.

Taking the time to negotiate:
* takes the win/lose out of the situation – everyone gains
* increases trust and willingness to co-operate; when people know you'll listen to them, they'll listen to you, and when you do have to say no they'll accept it was for a good reason and that you will agree to something they want another day

* increases mutual understanding and reduces frustration; taking your time and showing respect lowers the temperature and helps others to ask questions and listen in a calm atmosphere
* sets up a format for dealing with disagreements and conflict; once you have tried it and it has worked, you all know the rules for subsequent discussions and agreements.

You may think, particularly in your role as a parent, you shouldn't be negotiating as it shows weakness and parents should always be in charge. The reality is that negotiation is always more effective than one person giving orders, and is the assertive option. Saying 'Because I say so!' may work with small children. As they grow up, it becomes less effective. So how can you negotiate?

The key rules for negotiating are:

Talk when everyone is calm

Pick a neutral space and a time. If this is a family discussion, choose a time when everyone is relaxed such as over a family meal or a cup of coffee. Aim to give each of you time to have your say and listen to the other side without feeling rushed or pressured. Deferring the discussion until you're in a neutral spot also gives you the chance to think it through beforehand. For example, if your son says 'I'm not doing homework tonight!', or your mother calls and says 'It's a family Sunday lunch this week!', or a friend says 'I need you to look after my toddler for me this afternoon!' you *act*, don't react. Open the door to negotiation by acknowledging what has been said in a neutral way: 'You don't want to do homework/You want us to come for Sunday lunch this weekend/You want me to look after Fred this afternoon. Let's get a cup of coffee/make supper/give me ten minutes and I'll call you back, and we'll sit down and discuss it.' Stay non-committal and take the time you need to think about how you feel.

Gather information

Once everyone is sitting down ask for more information and listen. Take time to think about how you feel about the situation and what information you need to make your decision. If they are pushing you for an answer, say that you can give them a 'No' quickly, but if they want your agreement to something, you need time to talk it through.

Listen to the other person's views as well

In a discussion to reach a settlement that everyone is happy with it's important that both sides feel they have been heard, even if they don't get all that they want. Swap between listening and acknowledging the other person's feelings and needs, and stating your own. When making your feelings known, use 'I' messages to put your point across. Instead of saying 'No!' or 'I hate doing that!' say 'I can see what you're saying/asking but it doesn't suit me at the moment.' Be prepared to hear the other person's feelings and needs underneath their words. It may be 'I'm just not in a fit state after school to do my homework, I need a break!' or 'I'm really missing you and need some company' or 'I'm at the end of my tether!'

Be clear about what is (and is not) negotiable

You might like to make it clear from the start what issues you can and will budge on – and those that you can't and won't. Dropping other important commitments just because the person demanding your attention feels their needs are more important may not work for you. Accepting any relaxation on safety or health rules could be something non-negotiable. So too may be avoiding homework simply because they don't feel like doing it, or your helping out because your friend fancies yet another day off to go shopping.

Pick your battles

When you negotiate, focus on the issues that really matter. If you let go on small things you can stand firm when you need to. Negotiating takes time and can feel messy while you are in the middle of it. You may find yourself thinking 'I can't be bothered with this.' But negotiating is actually quicker than a whole saga of shouting, slamming down phones, sulking, and having feuds. You may be tempted to think 'It was so much simpler when I insisted – or gave in for a quiet life!' It might have been simpler, but it was far less pleasant in the long run as resentment and frustration spoiled the atmosphere.

Make an agreement

Once you've gathered in all the information you need, heard the feelings and opinions of the other person and been satisfied they have heard yours too, come to an agreement. Sometimes a conflict is about needs and beliefs. For example, you and your mother may never agree that every adult child still has to come to Sunday lunch every week or your teenager and you that homework is a waste of time. What you can do is discuss and agree to differ on your opposing beliefs, then negotiate agreements around behaviour so that important needs of everyone can be met with some compromise: 'OK – no homework tonight/until you've had a chance to recharge. But it has to be done so what we've agreed is you'll do it later/tomorrow.' Or 'Love you Mum but this weekend is for us as a family. I'll ring you on Monday and we'll fix up coming next weekend. Why don't you call that friend of yours?'

Check out that the agreement meets your and the other person's needs and that the outcome is acceptable to you both. And check out that you both have the same understanding of what has been agreed. One way of doing this is to have a contract. State clearly – or even write down – exactly what you and the other person have said will be done. Work out a fair exchange and one that you can both agree on. Make a precise record of the decision, including:

* what you've both agreed to do
* how you have agreed to do it
* when you have agreed to do it by
* for how long you have agreed to do this.

Review agreements regularly

Review such arrangements regularly. If the terms of the agreement are not being met, discuss why and whether the contract needs to be redrawn or whether something needs to be adjusted. When you're getting used to being assertive and so are the people around you, they might slip back into old habits, or even feel the need to test boundaries from time to time. Be prepared to stand firm unless it's time to review the agreement.

Say thank you!

Everyone co-operates when they feel good about it. The more comfortable you become with being assertive, the more confident and self-assured you are, the better other people will also feel about the relationships they have with you. If you thank them for co-operating, and frequently tell them you appreciate what they are doing, they have every incentive for repeating that behaviour. Whether it is family, friends or work colleagues, if most of your encounters are positive and enabling rather than hostile or conflicted you give them a motivation for wanting to interact in this way with you rather than it being a power struggle. If you share opinions in a positive, caring atmosphere when you do need to resolve an issue, the practice gained in being positive helps you to focus on feelings and needs, and swap between listening and expressing yourself, on the route to a resolution.

Teaching and modelling assertiveness skills can make family life so much easier for everyone. When children squabble what often happens is they come to you, to be referee or to manage the negative emotions for them. When you continually act as the mediator, settling the rows, this means they never have to learn how to cope for themselves. It works far better to hand over responsibility to them.

* State the problem – 'I see two children arguing over which programme to watch.'
* State your expectation – 'I think you can sort this out yourselves in a way that suits you both.'
* State what will happen – 'I'm going to leave you here and you'll come to me in ten minutes and tell me what you've agreed between you.'

If they can't agree, send them back again. Point out nobody wins if they can't agree, and that it must be a mutually satisfying arrangement.

You'll be surprised how often kids at loggerheads once expected to negotiate and compromise will do so. It's all in the expectation!